The Secrets of Seduction
from Regency England's
Most Eligible Bachelor

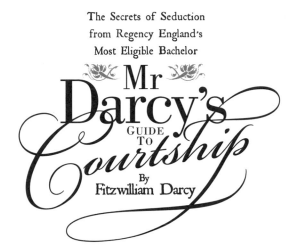

Mr
Darcy's
GUIDE
TO
Courtship

By
Fitzwilliam Darcy

Published in Great Britain in 2013 by Old House books & maps, Midland House, West Way, Botley, Oxford OX2 0PH, United Kingdom.

4301 21st Street, Suite 220B. Long Island City, NY 11101, USA.

Website: www.oldhousebooks.co.uk

A CIP catalogue record for this book is available from the British Library.

ISBN: 978 1 90840 259 2

Emily Brand has asserted her right under the Copyright, Designs and Patents Act, 1988, to be identified as the author of this book.

Printed in China through Worldprint Ltd.

13 14 15 16 17 10 9 8 7 6 5 4 3 2 1

Illustrations are acknowledged as follows:

The Bridgeman Art Library, pages 8, 42 and 61; The Lewis Walpole Library, Yale University, pages 10, 18, 27, 52, 62, 68, 99, 102, 106, 120, 128, 170, 175, 198, 203 and 205; Library of Congress, pages 20, 41, 122, 127 and 140; Mary Evans Picture Library, pages 143, 150, 152, 165 and 208.

Original artwork on pages 188, 189, 190, 191 and 192 courtesy of Mr Adrian Teal.

The remaining images are from the author's collection.

Cover art by Miss Merlyn Harvey

Designed by Mr S. Larking

ACKNOWLEDGEMENTS

Miss Brand respectfully dedicates this work to Mrs Lowell Black and Mrs Susheela Crease - matchless tutors in the feminine arts of seduction - in recognition of their work as honourable co-founders of the TWC, London's most exclusive society for the effective implementation of those arts.

With special thanks to Mr Tim Bullamore for his editorial expertise, and to Mr Abraham Davies for tolerating Mr Darcy's intrusion into our lives with admirable fortitude.

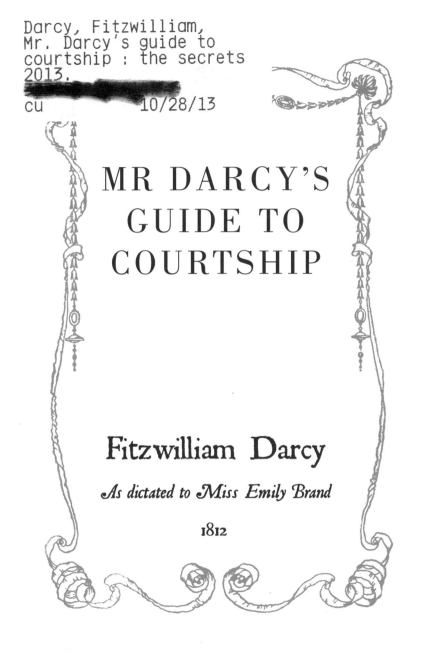

MR DARCY'S
GUIDE TO
COURTSHIP

Fitzwilliam Darcy

As dictated to Miss Emily Brand

1812

Dedicated to Mr. Charles Bingley.
May this cure you once and for all of your
utterly disastrous taste in females.

To Court. *v.a* [from the noun.]
To woo; to solicit a woman to marriage.

- Dr Johnson's *Dictionary*, 1755

PREFACE

THE modern modes of courtship being, as they are, perfectly abominable, I am convinced that no apology is required for the publication of this small volume on the subject. The unbridled improprieties daily to be observed in the conduct of young lovers are manifest even in the most fashionable circles, rendering many otherwise amiable creatures as disgusting to society as they are dangerous to themselves. These counsels were originally composed for the benefit of an esteemed friend, whose virtuous heart, open countenance, and almost cretinous inability to detect a lady of dubious intentions have conspired to disappoint him in affairs of the heart three times in as many months. In making them available to a general audience I hope to restore some decorum to modern romance, and to show how amorous addresses may efficiently and successfully be brought to a conclusion.

I presume that no introduction as to the particulars of my character and social standing are required, and I shall not waste my time and ink in relaying them. My repose being relentlessly disturbed by the swoons of passing ladies, I have long suspected that something in my countenance is irresistibly pleasing to the fairer sex. I flatter myself that being in possession of noble blood, a considerable estate, and being generally owned to be the most eligible bachelor in Derbyshire - in short a gentleman of *great parts* - I am quite qualified to pen a few short words on this delicate subject. Indeed, undisturbed as I am by the burdens attending the maintenance of a wife, I believe I shall suffer no check to the strength of my genius from beginning to end.

I am not at all solicitous to know whether the reader likes it or not; I am quite confident that it will commend itself to men and women of *understanding*, and therefore whosoever dislikes it deserves no claim to that title. I certainly have no reason to make apologies for the imbecility of my reader.

F. Darcy

February 1812

PREFACE

TO THE SECOND EDITION

AS GOOD WINE needs no bush, so neither does this second edition of *Mr Darcy's Guide to Courtship* stand in need of a commendatory epistle. The remarkable quality of the insights afforded by the original volume precluded any personal astonishment at the violence of the popular response, but I admit to being rather ill-prepared for the disorder that has rained down on Pemberley in the intervening months.

I have been deluged with letters from my readers – some noble and many, regrettably, vulgar – seeking advice on how they may better conduct their amours. Although I care not for indulging the whims of the common rabble, yet I will attempt to be civil to those who could at least construct a tolerable sentence: I conclude this revised edition with a selection of the complaints, to which is added my own honest counsel, and I trust that this puts an end to the matter. All missives received henceforth shall be promptly and unceremoniously dispatched to the fire.

F. Darcy

September 1812

CONTENTS

Editor's Note: There are some errata in this book, but the Author says he is too busy and important to give you a note of them.

CHAPTER I

Romance in the Regency Era

MATRIMONY is a kind of lottery, wherein there are as many blanks as there are prizes. The romancers of this world would have you believe that where the yearnings of the heart are concerned, we all have a better guide in ourselves than any other person can be. I must undeceive you of this preposterous notion. In truth, there is no better guide than *this book*. I congratulate you for advancing your cause so unreservedly by your purchase of it.

The lower classes have grown rather fond of bemoaning their wants of freedom, but the ill effects of a bad matrimonial bargain will in fact be felt more keenly by persons of quality. While the unrefined feel at liberty to forget propriety (and the law) so far as to 'sell' their spouses for half a crown and a pint of ale if the whim takes them, a *gentleman* must bury all thought of an unsightly wife with fine feasts, mistresses, the opera and vast quantities of brandy. One wonders, frankly, why the common herd complain so vociferously when they know nothing of the trials their betters endure. But I digress.

As the early season of courtship is crucial in determining the potential success of a match, time should not be wasted in sighing, fainting away, refusing food or breaking into song. I shall proceed to acquaint the reader with the woeful state of ignorance that currently reigns, the dangers of a hasty alliance, and my own faultless reflections on what is termed 'love', the whole offering a complete picture of English amorous affairs in the year 1812.

NO MISSION BUT MATRIMONY

THE female inhabitants of this country labour under a general fixation with wedding bells. The mere mention of a wealthy bachelor is quite enough to send half a neighbourhood to distraction, and the prospect of his *presence* will transform a perfectly rational town into a giddy, giggling mass of new bonnets and ribbons. I can myself take complete credit for the recent revival of the economy of Lincoln, where proprietors of millinery and cosmetic tonics saw their income increase tenfold for the duration of my last visit. Not that the faces of its residents betrayed any benefit from the expense.

An eligible gentleman not in possession of a wife is assailed from every quarter with a fervour bordering on derangement. Once his fortune is heard of, general prejudice will turn so violently in his favour that it would be the death of the hopeful ladies to regard him as anything less than the handsomest man of their acquaintance. The notion of marriage may not have entered his head, and yet it is fixed in the schemes of every family he meets, and his repose will be disturbed not only by the single females but their mothers, fathers and friends; the very earth he treads wills him to select a wife from local stock. Until, of course, a man of greater standing comes to their notice.

But while the rational part of the world is uniformly beset by the sighs of ladies with no mission but securing a husband, it is most unfortunate in being simultaneously annoyed by melancholy gentlemen unequal to the task of wooing them. Lovers are, of all people, the most disagreeable. However, with study and proper regulation of sentiment, this ludicrous state of affairs may be easily resolved and courtship rendered a much less vexing exercise for all parties.

Who is permitted to derive benefit from this work?

LORDS and labourers alike are afflicted by the troubles of the heart. (I mean to make no compliment to the understanding of the latter, of course, but rather to acknowledge Cupid's regrettable embrace of egalitarianism.) Thus, while much of my advice is directed at the better sort of gentleman, I have no objection to persons of lesser cerebral attainment deriving benefit from it; that is to say, females, persons of trade, and the lower classes. I do, however, expect my readership to command certain levels of intelligence and moral feeling. If you are equivocal on either of these points then I beg you take your leave of this book; in the hands of a foolish or unscrupulous character, I fear that the potency of its wisdom would cause rather more ill than good.

Most particularly I urge rogues of all persuasions to seek inspiration for their idle gallantries elsewhere. To these incorrigible scoundrels, I say only this: any man who sports with a woman's feelings, or who pursues her with dishonourable intentions, is the last word in all that is caddish and bounderish. Save your ill-gotten earnings for John Thorpe's *Pleasures of Bath* and other lewd scrawls, busy yourself with fallen women and desist from corrupting the nation's stock of eligible females. Let that be an end to it.

I address only those who seek to make a successful and respectable courtship their object. Whether you do so for love or pecuniary advancement is no concern of mine (unless your impertinence stretches so far as to inspire designs upon my sister). Having been entirely untroubled by amatory failure, I cannot conceive of any defensible objection to the legitimacy of my counsel. I reflect with great satisfaction that at present, in common with a noted musician and philosopher, while I am beset by nigh on one hundred grievances, a vexatious female need not be counted among them.

On the Division between the Sexes

All persons of sound judgment have a duty to marry: men, to propagate their family line, and ladies, to relieve the financial burden from their parents. Couples unable to boast any portion of sense between them are permitted to increase their felicity through marriage, but in the interest of national security they ought to refrain from *breeding*.

The natural difference between the sexes - such as compels males to fight duels and females to enjoy embroidery and other trifling amusements - is displayed in the distinct role each assumes in courtship. In a logical division of labour, the gentleman - blessed with the larger share of reason - enjoys the advantage of selection. A woman, physically and mentally equipped for compliance, is generally at liberty only to exercise the power of refusal. As such, the former must master the principles of finding a suitable female, promptly securing her affections, and expressing his intentions. The latter must learn how to heighten her attractions without being taken for a harlot, and how to reject or receive attentions with propriety. Those performing their duties without due diligence exhibit the worst kind of gratuitous folly: such as can prove fatal not only to their own reputation, but to those of all connected with them.

On the Division between the Classes

All truly civilised persons must master the principles of proper comportment. Those of the middling ranks, with no small degree of impertinence, aim to emulate their betters. While I condemn such abominable presumption as people stepping out of their rank entirely, this work may be singularly instructive for those with aspirations to court *slightly* above their station.

Even those of the most uncouth situations are subject to similar, if less noble, fancies of the heart. While I am not entirely averse to the notion that people of all classes may glean some intelligence from this book, I have no inclination to expend effort on those who have not taken the time to learn to read. Thus, I shall not trouble myself with enquiring deeply into the courtship techniques of the uneducated classes, which seem to be primarily based on the exchange of worthless love tokens and an immoderate consumption of gin.

A Specimen of Cheapside Romance

ON WHY ROMANCE MUST
BE REGULATED

WHEN a young person begins to entertain the notion of seeking a partner, his head is often so full of fanciful expectations that he plunges recklessly into the character of a lover before considering how the romance ought to be regulated. Contrary to the common presumption that he is headed for a season of enchantment and emotional discovery, at no other time has a man more need to be strict in his manners, nor a lady to be careful in her conduct.

Securing an advantageous match is the only way that a daughter may be of real service to her parents, and is a financial imperative for a younger son with no prospect of inheriting the wealth to which he has grown accustomed. Very few can afford to marry without some attention to money, and fewer still possess such wealth as to court exactly where they please.

Courtship is a singularly complicated business. Each sex nurses its own little deceits, whereby a lady may encourage attentions she fully intends to disappoint, or a gentleman may drop all pretence of attachment once he tires of his scheme. People believing themselves to be 'in love' are generally altered into creatures so unhinged that they should not be trusted with making important decisions, particularly those upon which their future felicity depends so fully. Hasty decisions and unchecked passions lay the foundations for an ultimately disappointing - if not utterly miserable - marriage. Even more injurious to a lady's virtue and a gentleman's honour, the affair may be abandoned before improper relations can be clothed in the decency of wedlock.

The proper regulation of romantic matters is essential not only as a matter of preserving individual morality but of *national* well-being. In short, if my advice is ignored, this country will quickly degenerate into a nest of confusion, debauchery and misery, closely resembling that currently reigning in France.

VARIETIES OF LICENTIOUSNESS

In which unmentionable vices are mentioned, with such boldness as may astonish and offend those of nervous dispositions

I DARESAY this brief sketch of the nation's amorous affairs in 1812 will be enough to disgust any discerning observer. Adultery and divorce have polluted the shades of the noblest of English houses, common prostitutes drape themselves in finery and are celebrated as fashionable courtesans, and gentlemen glory in ruining female reputations. It is my decided opinion that this certain indescribable medley of coarse language and thinly veiled wantonness betrays the influence of the garrulous, mischievous foreigner, who has ever revelled in scenes of lawlessness. We shall stand for nothing of the sort here; we are English, after all, and must distract ourselves from our improper desires by contemplating the weather, fishing, writing angry letters and holding any invitation to unbridled pleasure in contempt.

On the vices of men

In modern universities – and it is most abominably apparent at Oxford – young gentlemen consider indolence and dissipation not only as worthy pursuits but as necessary ones. Exercises of the mind are neglected in favour of the local ale-house, spectator sports, gambling, and discussing the relative physical merits of their female acquaintances (one must hope that English gentlemen of future generations will abandon such lamentable modes of licentiousness). Fleeting dalliances are more the fashion than affectionate companionships and idle men, for want of more honourable employ, meditate the seduction of ladies for sport. They invariably end their days insane from syphilis or suffering death at the hands of some disgruntled husband.

Another increasingly common sight on English soil is a species of man whose only ideas centre on dress, dandyism and damned affectation. I know nothing of the internal constitution of these men, only that, aside from the ridiculous fripperies in which they adorn themselves, they do in most external attributes resemble normal gentlemen. Such wilful masquerade renders them all the more dangerous in the eyes of reasonable society.

On the improprieties of women

Ladies appear to have forgotten their place. We may of course lay some blame at the feet of Mary Wollstonecraft and her *creative* pronouncements on the rights of the female sex; no doubt we shall soon be pestered by the mewings of wives wanting their own property, or to vote; nay, women in parliament! It is vexing enough that the lower orders trouble us with such demands, without women joining the chorus. We may at least derive consolation from the fact that the whole business is so nonsensical that I daresay it shall sink into obscurity tolerably soon.

Some ladies actively pursue a career of vice. While I quite comprehend the necessity of certain female *professionals* to alleviate particular frustrations that an unmarried man may suffer, I am often astonished at the audacity of some among their ranks. At just fifteen, Harriette Wilson - a female now much in fashion, despite the fact that her family are of no consequence whatsoever - applied to a personage no less distinguished than the Prince of Wales, offering herself thus: "I am told that I am very beautiful, so perhaps you would like to see me." The application resulted in a ticket to the *beau monde* for Miss Wilson, but I daresay no-one shall ever take her as his *wife*.

THOUGHTS ON LOVE

A man of romantic sensibilities will argue that the fortuitous union of two hearts is the best possible scheme for morals, posterity and mutual happiness that could possibly be contrived. The notion of affection within marriage has gained such strength in recent years that *wives* have begun to pester their husbands for gifts and treats with as much enthusiasm as their *mistresses*. While it is quite natural that this new emphasis on tender feeling between couples should have been welcomed by the new generation, I daresay there are few philosophies in which so many different species of nonsense are collected than in that of the power of love.

Love alone does not make for a prudent marriage.

It has for centuries been considered a mental disease, and the union of two such violently unstable individuals will not form a very pleasing picture of conjugal harmony. At its most severe, the affliction specialises in depriving sensible men of their wits, compelling chaste maidens to abandon their inhibitions, and convincing sufferers of both sexes to act in such a wild and unbecoming manner as would disgrace one of Robert Peel's Tamworth pigs. Though it manifests itself in heavy sighs and the composition of nauseating poetry rather than putrid boils and sweating fevers, I daresay the effect is no less offensive for observers.

Affection should not be feigned where it is not felt.

If love does not blossom during courtship, it is unlikely that there should be an appearance of it after marriage. The ladies in particular are apt to fondly imagine that the hearts of anyone showing them attention must be entirely under their spell, and honesty on this score is imperative. A disavowal of genuine attachment may not always put paid to a match of convenience; the lady will appreciate your candour and unless she is of an incurably silly disposition she will proceed to consider your suit on your other merits.

Love is not an all-consuming force of nature.

It does not subject the soul to uncontrollable ecstasies one moment and tortured frenzies the next; neither will a disappointed lover be obliged to nurse a broken heart until their inevitable, untimely death. The flagrancy with which 'free love' is now practised in certain literary quarters rather proves that the submission to emotions is far more likely to loosen one's morals than feed a happy marriage. The worst offenders, unfortunately, appear to view themselves as commendable disrupters of the established order and champions of progressive thought.

ARE YOU SUFFICIENTLY PREPARED?

EXHIBITING your preference for one person above all others is tantamount to a declaration of love, and onlookers will begin to plan your nuptials before you have so much as enquired into the lady's monetary prospects.

A note on age

Thoughts of courtship should only be entertained at a suitable age. Those too young for the venture indulge in rampant recklessness, and persons too old are bound for disappointment. A man of breeding may be considered of prime marriageable age at around twenty-eight and a lady at around twenty-two (by which time the financial affairs of the former may be tolerably well established, and the latter has had opportunity to lose the vestiges of youthful silliness). In England those below the age of one and twenty must obtain parental consent in order to wed by licence. Each year couples attempting to evade this convention by elopement make haste towards Gretna Green, but I daresay a marriage contracted in Scotland has never been such a one as young females dream of. Among the peasantry it is the custom to wed earlier, presumably as, in general, their careless lifestyle choices lead to an earlier grave.

The question of timing is critical for the fair sex, whose charms deteriorate so rapidly as they approach the years of danger that a lady may find herself rejecting suitors with alacrity one season and quite ignored the next. Such foolish behaviour yields a new crop of old maids each year.

However, age alone is not enough to prepare one for the trials that inevitably come with romantic intimacy - one must also be possessed of a certain maturity of mind, and strength of character. Seven years of instruction would be insufficient to prepare some for dealings with the opposite sex, yet seven days seem to be enough for others.

Assessing your readiness for romance

If you are contemplating courtship for the first time, some inquiry must be made into your readiness for embarking on this new and perilous stage of life. It is essential that you consider each of the following questions carefully and honestly - particularly if you are not blessed with the guidance of sensible parents.

Questions for the Gentlemen

1. How do you plan to support a family?

a) From my own independent income.

b) My father has supported me all these years, I daresay there is no need for him to stop now.

c) Love should be the primary concern in a marriage; material wealth is quite irrelevant.

d) Oh, my wife shall bring the fortune, I expect. I give no thought to financial affairs.

2. Are you well travelled?

a) I received a most enlightening education during my recent Grand Tour of Italy.

b) I have visited Cornwall with my family of late, but I did not think it as nice as Scarborough.

c) I take great pleasure in riding about the wild moors in the rain.

d) I prefer not to venture far. I suffer from terrible travel sickness, even in a barouche.

3. How would you describe your ideal day?

a) Up at six, dressed, shaved, breakfasted. Write letters for two hours, shooting, dinner, conclude the day with reading.

b) Anything to escape my tedious studies. It is all a terrible bore.

c) Gazing at nature's beauty, and reflecting on the tragical nature of the human condition.

d) I am more inclined to eating than sleeping, and more inclined to drinking than either.

4. Whom do you most admire?

a) William Pitt the Younger, a believer in sensible policies for a happier Britain.

b) Oh Lord Nelson, the greatest of our military heroes! How brave he was!

c) Lord Byron. He comprehends what it means to be truly in love.

d) Beau Brummell. The man polishes his boots with champagne!

5. What is the principal function of a wife?

a) A partner to support one through life, and provider of children.

b) Father won't let me have a dog. He is allergic.

c) A kindred soul, a lover, the one to whom one gives the *key to one's heart*.

d) She must be an excellent maker of pies.

Questions for the Ladies

1. Are you at least one and twenty?

a) Yes.

b) Oh, almost!

c) What does age matter where love is concerned?

d) A man who would ask a lady to confess her age is the worst kind of brute!

2. Are you a burden to your parents?

a) Yes, although I contribute to household economy however I can.

b) Oh no, we are a merry lot! Mama would be quite forlorn without me!

c) It is more irksome for *me*; the yearnings of my soul shall never be satisfied within these four walls!

d) I do not live with them - in fact my true parentage is something of a mystery.

3. Are you considered accomplished?

a) I am proficient in languages, drawing, embroidery, music, dancing, poetry, and plenty more besides.

b) My governess tells me I should have a fine singing voice, if only I would take the time to practise.

c) I prefer the more expressive arts, above all music and poetry.

d) Oh, I daresay I execute most things very ill, but inflict my efforts upon the public at every opportunity.

4. Who should you most like to be?

a) Queen Charlotte, a faithful wife who gladly provided her husband with fifteen children.

b) Charlotte, Princess of Wales — what a fine joke it should be to be heir to the throne and have one's pick of *all the princes*!

c) Sarah Siddons, the finest tragic actress of our age. When she played Isabella her audience were rendered so melancholy they couldn't even applaud!

d) Oh, any of the fashionable ladies at Court! I should so like to have such a pretty set of gowns.

5. What is your preferred reading material?

a) Anything that may serve to improve my understanding.

b) Something shockingly wicked like Mrs Radcliffe's *The Mysteries of Udolpho* (as long as papa doesn't find out).

c) Shakespeare's *Sonnets*.

d) Oh I don't see any point in reading, I had much rather go shopping.

Mostly As: You are sufficiently prepared. You may proceed to capture the hearts of suitable persons.

Mostly Bs: Your youthful exuberance may be pleasing to some, but your immaturity of mind will be your undoing. I advise you to wait a little longer, and stop reading silly novels, before attempting courtship.

Mostly Cs: Your romantic notions put you in danger of contracting a highly unsuitable match. If you do not learn to exercise sense over sensibility, your unruly passions will lead you astray.

Mostly Ds: You are far too ridiculous. You are permitted to marry, if you are of age, and if someone will have you; but I would advise against breeding.

CAUTIONARY NOTES,
FOR GENTLEMEN

WHEN King George enquired of his minister William Pitt the Younger why he had not yet thought of marriage, the response was: "I have never yet had time, Sire." Pitt's critics are fond of joking that he gained more pleasure from a glass of port than he ever could from a woman, but I suspect that he was simply well-acquainted with the fact that courting a lady is a time-consuming and costly business.

For the benefit of gentlemen unsure of the expenses ordinarily attending married life, I include an inquiry into the subject, published in 1780, in order to highlight those costs usually disregarded until one's wife has entirely disposed of the contents of one's coffers.

The Bachelor's Monitor

Being a proper calculation of the expenses usually attending the maintenance of a wife and children

This estimate supposes that the married man receives £2,000 with his wife; and has, in the compass of fifteen years, eight children; four of whom die, and four only are alive at one time. In this case, if he lives with tolerable elegance, his expenses will be nearly as follows per annum, viz:

	l	s	d
House-rent at 40l, taxes, ward and parish rates, and pew in the church	49	0	0
Wages of two maid servants, and one man in livery	22	0	0
Fitting up the house at Madam's desire	22	10	0
Repairs, alterations, white-washing &c, every fourth year	5	0	0
Butcher, fishmonger, baker, cheesemonger, brewer, grocer &c	131	0	0
Wine, Cyder, Rum, Brandy, Cordial-waters	35	0	0
Tea, chocolate, coffee &c	20	0	0
Washing & laundry business, with soap, starch &c	25	0	0

Physician, surgeon, apothecary (if Madam be vapourish or fanciful, it will be much more for herself and children)	12	o	o
Christmas donations fitting for a housekeeper	3	o	o
Confectioner & pastry cook for jellies, conserves, sweetmeats &c	5	o	o
Perfumer, for essences, lavender water, washes, snuff &c	3	o	o
Draper, Milliner, Shoe makers, hosier, long & costly train of ribbons, muslins and bonnets	90	o	o
Madam's pocket expenses throughout the year, for coach-hire, chair-hire, visiting, & for going to Operas, Balls, publick spectacles & feasts, Vauxhall Gardens &c	40	o	o

Expenses attending the arrival of children (average per annum):

Lyings-in, eight in fifteen years, christenings, midwife, nurse, hysteric water &c	5	o	o
If but four children living at one time, there must be four funerals	2	o	o
The nursing, wet or dry, of the children	18	o	o
Schooling, even in infancy, and necessary articles	10	o	o

Education of four surviving children as they grow up, supposing dancing, writing, casting accounts (not including feminine studies such as music, and French)	15	0	0
The baby catalogue, viz: child-bed basket, fine satin mantle and sleeves for the Christening, Cradle, Headbands, caps, short & long-stays, shoes, neckcloths, cap and feather, cloak, anodyne necklace and other infant medicines	10	10	0
Total	522	20	0

Probable expenses, not brought into the Account:

- Country-house, or Lodgings, Journeys to Bath, Tunbridge, Scarborough; Chaise and horses; saddle-horse for little excursions, Riding-habits, Card-playing (an amusement that has banished the needle and other useful employments out of the modern education for ladies).

- Presents, such as watch and equipage, jewels, laces, rings &c. Perhaps lap-dogs, parrots, canary-birds &c.

- To say nothing of the Chance of *Feminine Extravagance,* which we shall forbear to mention out of Tenderness to the Ladies.

- Plays & pocket expenses of the man are likewise excluded.

All considered, it must be own'd, that the above estimate affords a very melancholy prospect to one, who is a well-wisher to the state of matrimony.

CAUTIONARY NOTES, FOR LADIES

IN a generous fit of egalitarian spirit I include for the instruction of my female readers a remarkably vehement defence of the unmarried lady, in a letter penned by a young noblewoman of Highbury and recently published in a London newspaper.

An Apology for Single Ladies.
By Miss Emma Woodhouse.

Sir,

I had the recent misfortune of reading your article proclaiming marriage to be the only desirable path for a woman to take in life. You insist that "Ladies should think themselves under great obligations to gentlemen who will marry them despite their faults" – insufferable! – and your impertinence in presuming that every woman is ready to accept anybody who asks for her hand – unpardonable! A pitiable picture of female prospects indeed!

As I make the affairs of the heart my most particular study, I must object most heartily. Must a lady submit to the first here-and-therian who pays her his addresses? Must she marry a man merely because she is asked, or because he is attached to her, and can express himself tolerably well? The answer is no – even if he is mightily good-looking.

A woman makes many sacrifices when she marries: she forsakes her own friends and family; she gives up her very name, to build up a husband's property, and propagate a name not her own. I daresay many would chuse to live single and independent, were it not for the annoying oaths and flatteries of men. I should like to see all men suffer as violent an interrogation as I am determined to inflict upon any suitor!

You also imply that wives derive pleasure only from pestering their husbands for pets and treats. Is she not entitled to some small comforts when he has possession of her entire fortune to dispose of at his pleasure? If a lady's spouse gives her reason to love him, I assure you, sir, that she may be content with no parrots or canary-birds but her children, nor any lap-dog but her husband!

A single woman of good fortune – for whom real love can be the only inducement to marry – may be as sensible and pleasant as anybody else. Of course, on the question of Old Maids, there is as much difference between the genteel and the working-class mind as there is between the fashionable milliner's show-room and a horse's stable. *A* fine joke it would be for an impoverished spinster to be so fastidious! *A* narrow income does so contract the mind that such a woman could not hope to be held in anything but the contempt of her betters.

In all, my observation of the world has proved to me so forcibly the miseries of two people of contrary characters torturing each other to the end of their natural lives that I can see little reason to take up the experiment. Thus concludes my defence of the independent lady.

Yours,
EW.

MARRIAGE: AN AFFAIR OF NATIONAL IMPORTANCE

AN unfortunate match, badly handled, will not only render you both miserable, but also cast a shadow over your families and general acquaintance - even the country at large. As a rule, I urge only the most reasonable men and women of this generation to become the parents of the next. We have no right to bequeath to it an inheritance of woe in the form of silly, scandalised parents and such stupid offspring as they are bound to produce.

If the parents are persons of distinction, the portion of sense allotted to their children can amount to an issue of *national importance.* As disturbing as it may be to reflect upon the notion of today's politicians as dribbling babes, those with aspirations to a career in government do not simply emerge from Cambridge or Oxford as fully formed political creatures; they must be born and raised along with the rest of us, and it is imperative that parliament is not entirely populated by those who have inherited the dull wits, as well as the titles, of their ancestors. Allowing an utter blockhead to dress as an educated gentleman and take the reins of government is folly indeed.

For the royal family, of course, the intended parties are rarely trusted with the power of choice. Some are more gracious about the situation than others. King George III dutifully embraced his politically convenient but plain-faced wife, while his son the Regent has been so publicly displeased with his own match that she threatens to quit the country entirely. His Highness does not seem overly distressed by it.

To avoid unnecessary displays of emotion, all men and women entering the field of courtship must be sensible of their responsibilities and prepare for every eventuality. The essential rules run thus:

1. Ensure that you are not utterly disgusting to behold
2. Make certain that (s)he is qualified for the post
3. Express feelings with propriety, at a suitable juncture
4. Uphold your promises

The subsequent chapters reveal the most effective methods of amorous attack during every stage on the road to matrimony, the whole containing ample and interesting instruction to both sexes, which I am certain - if punctually followed - cannot fail of securing uninterrupted contentment and satisfaction to all reasonable parties.

CHAPTER II

Making Oneself Agreeable

MANY suitors discover too late the unfortunate truth that first impressions imprint steadfastly in the breast. At every public appearance, all aspects of your person - your posture, the stateliness of your brow and the sweetness of your odour - will be laid under scrutiny. On occasion, one may even be subjected to positively *lurid* examinations of the cut of one's breeches or the shapeliness of one's calves.

Depending on the offence, a bad opinion formed on early acquaintance can be utterly irreparable - an ill-timed bodily emission, or the convulsive termination of a well-modulated laugh with an ungracious snort, can kill a promising inclination stone dead. An attractive stranger with grace, wit and a well-tailored coat will be more favourably received than a malodorous, lolloping lord with unfashionable *mustachios* - perhaps even *after* he is revealed to be no more distinguished than an upstart candle-maker.

To proceed promptly to the matter of your instruction, I shall first offer hints to the ladies, and then disclose how a gentleman may heighten his physical attractions. Whatever your rank or sex, I implore you to study the relevant sections well before disgusting any noble personage with the dubious pleasure of your acquaintance.

PART ONE:

HINTS TO THE LADIES

IT may be generally observed that ladies are more keenly governed by a sense of their duty to make themselves pleasing to the opposite sex. At its most powerful, this fascination with cosmetic affairs is manifested in a refusal to quit the house before carefully weighing the merits of at least fifteen different gowns, and an almost maniacal enthusiasm for the acquisition of shoes.

On the Lamentable Preponderance of Plain Women

Regrettably, such fastidiousness rarely guarantees pleasing results. Even in a fashionable ballroom, of a hundred ladies present perhaps five will be grotesque, five and twenty decidedly ugly, forty disfigured by poor taste, twenty may be owned tolerable, ten agreeable and hardly one truly beautiful. One wonders at the boldness with which they dare to appear in society in such a miserable state.

The number of plain women is possibly the most forcible argument against visiting the country, where they are even more vexingly out of proportion. When obliged to take a promenade through one of the less sophisticated towns - such as Newcastle, or Doncaster - one may observe each handsome female face followed by thirty frights, one after another. Sometimes *one hundred* may pass by with hardly a tolerable face among them! Certainly one will find nothing in their features marking a woman of distinguished birth. While I condemn those wheedling arts employed by many ladies for captivation, an utter incapability of making oneself pleasing to the opposite sex is quite a repulsive failure in a woman. However, the mysteries of feminine beauty being no fit subject for a gentleman to dwell upon, I am glad to hand the task over to Miss Caroline Bingley. Having by no means exhausted herself in hovering over my writing desk, nor in her *indefatigable* admiration of my handwriting, Miss Bingley has rather *insisted* on making some small contribution to this work.

Feminine Beauty
What it is, and How to Retain it

Hints from Miss Caroline Bingley

RELUCTANT as I first was to reveal the secrets of the fashionable feminine *toilette* to all and sundry, I am pleased to lay them before you at the particular request of the most excellent Mr Darcy, whom I trust would never be such an unconscionable brute as to abuse the opportunity of studying such intimate information himself (really, sir, you are *shocking!*).

The present generation is to be congratulated for its rejection of the monstrous fashions of our grandmothers, whose towering masses of hair and ridiculous hoop petticoats could barely be gathered into an opera box (quite *what* was thought attractive about such deformed figures one simply cannot make out). The modern beauty exhibits more grace and enjoys more comfort. While it is true that the extent of our loveliness does depend more heavily upon our natural charms, physical imperfections may be significantly reduced by a few delicate arts.

Being peculiarly fortunate in my portion of natural beauty, I flatter myself that I need not have recourse to many of the measures outlined below. Yet I do pity the greater part of the feminine world, which must employ all paltry devices at their disposal to pass as barely tolerable! While there are many vicious ladies who seek to recommend their own charms by undervaluing the accomplishments of others, I trust that my disclosure of such invaluable secrets shall testify to my real concern to help those less happily situated than myself, and allow them to aspire to my own level of elegance, even if they have no real hopes of achieving it.

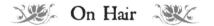 ## On Hair

- A fine head of hair has long been viewed as one of the most distinguished natural ornaments we can possess. It should be combed off the forehead and arranged in ringlets at the sides. Under no circumstances have it dressed it so that it falls in heavy locks over the forehead and eyes: this is a custom totally at variance with every principle of good taste and, as well as being destructive to every kind of beauty, it betrays a wretched lower-middle class imitation of gentility.

- The hair must be sufficiently clean: in the morning, apply a paste of the whites of six eggs to the head and leave to dry. Rinse with a mixture of rum and rose-water, in equal quantities.

- Preserve the lustre of hair with ointments such as *Atkinson's Bear Grease*, or make your own pomade at home. Simply order your maid to prepare a mixture of beef marrow, brandy and unsalted lard (although veal fat may do just as well), and apply liberally for an unparalleled shine.

- An embarrassing encounter with a particularly hirsute gentlewoman in York convinces me that the unseemly subject of superfluous hair cannot be omitted. Outbreaks of this sort on the arms, neck and face must be promptly removed. *Hubert's Roseate Powder* is quite fit for the purpose.

The cultivation of superfluous hair is not to be recommended

On Imperfections of the Skin

- Keep one's skin fashionably pale by taking care to avoid venturing out of doors without one's bonnet, gloves or parasol. Thoughtless ladies who allow themselves to be knocked about and exposed to every sort of weather until they are not fit to be seen, are no more likely to be admired than a country milkmaid.

- Freckles may be removed with lotions of lead – such as *Bloom of Ninon* – which bestow upon the skin a pretty kind of delicate fairness. The more potent varieties do have a tendency to temporarily paralyse the face, and so should not be applied immediately before making your face available to public view.

- Unsightly eruptions on the face are the source of much disgust. They may be treated with *Gowland's Lotion,* a mercury paste. As this does have an unfortunate tendency to burn sensitive skin clean off, the more cautious may prefer *eau de veau:* have a servant boil a calf's foot in river water, add rice, white bread, butter and eggs, and distil the whole in a bottle of boiling water. Apply to face with all due delicacy.

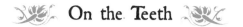 On the Teeth

- The beauty of the teeth consists in their arrangement, regularity and brilliance; the latter, at least, we may endeavour to perfect without resorting to surgical procedure. There are many varieties of tooth-paste, usually based in pulverised charcoal, soot, brick-dust, honey or - most effective of all - sulphuric acid.

- The best implement for cleaning the mouth is a tooth-brush of root of marsh-mallow. A rinse of lemon juice, oil of bergamot and claret should be used daily, for freshness of breath and to fasten loose teeth.

- If your teeth are beyond repair, apply to a dental surgeon in London, who can offer substitutes crafted from whalebone, or donor teeth pulled from the mouths of the lower classes, if you have no objection to the thought of having your mouth thus defiled. I confess I would incline to the former - efforts to uphold estimable standards of decorum may be more easily detected among the whale community than among the London poor, I have little doubt.

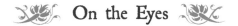 # On the Eyes

- If one keeps late hours, the eyes will droop and take on a greyish hue. Simply retire for a short while, and allow the gentlemen to lament your absence. Alternatively, eye lotions such as *Olympia Dew* can restore a seductive sparkle.

- The recent military campaigns in Egypt have enlivened enthusiasm for ancient cosmetic fashions, and some ladies now apply black pastes of oiled soot or burnt cork around their eyelashes and brows. Subtle colouring *may* be tolerated - if your complexion permits it - but persons indulging in such reckless folly as to wear eye *liner* are generally presumed to be brazen harlots or unqualified lunatics.

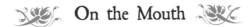 On the Mouth

- The beauty of the mouth is peculiarly necessary to constitute a fine face. The lower lip ought to be fuller than the upper, in order to give an elegant rounding to the chin. The same effect may be achieved by perfecting a gentle pout, but practise is crucial. Innumerable young ladies - who would otherwise have been passable - ruin their prospects entirely by overzealously thrusting out their lips at every male in the vicinity, with all the refinement of a Billingsgate trout.

- A natural ruby tint to the lips is prized, but this depends largely on the good health of the lady. The application of vermilion, or red paint, remains the preserve of actresses and other women of loose virtue.

On Ageing with Grace

- Beyond the age of five and twenty, a lady must accept the loss of her bloom of youth. For those of advanced years to pass themselves off as sprightly maids of nineteen is not only a vain enterprise, but one inexpressibly distasteful to all who are forced to witness it.

- To reduce wrinkling of the skin, liberally smear the juice of a green pineapple, or alternatively that of a raw onion, over the face each night.

- If your appearance is truly offensive, you may be permitted to consider the application of a little cosmetic paint. White paints for the skin are acknowledged to be ruinous to health – causing such annoyance as to bring on paralytic spasms, premature death, &c – but the occasional use of rouge may be tolerated; yet it is only tolerated, and is never pleasing. A violently rouged woman is one of the most disgusting objects to the eye. Such measures are highly unlikely to recommend you to the opposite sex, but if you must venture into public view you may at least shield persons of fragile sensibilities from your natural unsightliness.

On Slenderness of Form

- As modern fashions have a tendency to render one's figure quite visible, it is of the utmost importance to afford it some attention. Moderation is vital: a preponderance of shapeless rolling flesh is generally allowed to be displeasing, but too willowy a form confers upon one a sickly air of consumption that will never be owned fashionable.

- As an active lifestyle is hardly appropriate for a lady of elegance, violent physical exertion remains the preserve of the unrefined. Accordingly it is easy enough for the common sort of woman to avoid unflattering weight gain – though many are rather apt to be too thin – but ladies of quality are forced to be more ingenious in their methods of taking exercise.

- Pursuits acceptable in one's juvenile years are unbecoming in adulthood. Only very young ladies may seek recreation in healthful sports such as shuttlecocks, the see-saw and hide-and-seek.

- Exercise may be obtained on horseback, or in a carriage if the weather is unfavourable. Rubbing of the skin is an excellent substitute for exercise, when that is impracticable.

- Take a daily turn about the house rather than venturing out of doors, where the elements will conspire to derange the hair and flush the cheeks.

- A gentle morning walk can be beneficial: country air is an excellent bracer of the nerves, but only when breathed at proper hours.

- Though at the time it may be refreshing and agreeable, physical exertion will in the end prove destructive to your constitution, as well as provoke attacks of perspiration and reddening of the face; the whole unquestionably producing anything but a pleasing effect.

 ## On Fragrance

- No matter how ardently you are admired from afar, once one comes into close proximity to a suitor there is nothing more likely to repulse his advances than an unfeminine fragrance. To promote cleanliness as well as preserving one's health, there is nothing preferable to bathing. By regular ablutions, corporeal impurities are thrown off and the body is kept sweet-smelling.

- Heavy perfumes are no longer acceptable, but splashing oneself with essence of lavender water will do, if one has not time for full bodily immersion.

⊰ On Fashion ⊱

- Fine taste in apparel is a certain indicator of persons of quality, while a careless style of dress betrays lax manners. The general scarcity of good taste outside of London is easily discerned at country balls, which are so full of ladies too stout for their gowns that one might fancy oneself gawping at pigs in a pen.

- Let your style of dress always be appropriate to the hour of the day.

- Wearing gossamer dresses with bare necks and arms, in a hard frost, has become the mode in this country. Comfort must be sacrificed for fashion, even if we lay ourselves open to the ravages of rheumatisms, palsies and early death – how else shall we get a husband?

- The colours for young persons, when not white, should be tender shades of green, yellow, pink, blue and lilac. Those of majestic deportment may choose fuller shades, perhaps wearing precious stones and feathered plumes if their rank permits it.

- Consult *La Belle Assemblée* and the gossip columns of London newspapers to keep acquainted with current trends.

To be admitted truly elegant, a lady must be pleasing in her manners, her expression, her tone of voice, her lightness of foot, her conversation *&c &c*. Likewise, to be thought a beauty she must identify the faults of her face and form, and correct them. If even your best efforts are in vain, you need not absolutely despair of finding a passable sort of husband - from among the lesser clergy perhaps, or a man of trade. At public assemblies confine yourself to rooms with dim light, and be sure to keep company with ladies who are even more plain than yourself - your meagre charms will at least be accentuated by comparison.

I fear that if you still do not prevail, there is nothing more that you can hope to learn from,

Miss C. Bingley

BEHAVING LIKE A LADY

THE following treatise offers hints towards correcting your behaviour in the company of the superior sex. I am prepared to concede the possibility that - rather than your simply being monstrously unfashionable - your weaker feminine intellect may actually render you incapable of identifying your faults. Thus, I trust that some enlightenment from the masculine perspective cannot fail to be deemed agreeable. When in the presence of a gentleman, attend to the following rules at all times:

• There shall be no idle chatter or talking nonsense.

• Confine yourself to genteel topics of conversation. Do not presume to enter into discussions of politics or other masculine affairs. If a lady should have the misfortune of being better informed than her male companions, she should conceal as well as she can. Neither should she prattle about muslin and lace - however mortifying it may be to feminine feelings, the heart of a man is very little affected by the composition of a lady's attire; he is quite content to admire its effect.

• Improve your mind by extensive reading. It is undignified to offer opinions unsought, but some learning is practical if you find yourself bound to an unconquerably silly husband. I do not, of course, encourage the study of such lively *nonsense* as pours from the pens of most lady novelists.

• Avoid coarse and unseemly language. If you are a native of the north of England, you would do well to study elocution before horrifying your company and humiliating yourself with the vulgarity of your accent.

• Maintain command of your facial expressions at all times. Carelessness in this regard distorts a handsome face, and ruins entirely the aspect of a bad one. If you are in the undignified habit of grinning stupidly, your company will naturally presume that you have been too free with the punch and, worse, your charms be reduced to those of a wrinkled hag before you reach the age of five and twenty.

An example of admirable facial control

A lady trapped in a violent gurn

• This is to be particularly observed when exhibiting accomplishments. At the piano, women twist themselves into such contortions as would almost incline observers to conclude that they are suffering from the tooth-ache, or gout. Their heads swing, their eyes roll, they sigh and pant and seem ready to expire. What is this all about? They call it *expression*, but the fair warbler is more likely to arouse questions about the balance of her mind than admiration of her genius.

• Do not cast your eyes wantonly about, nor brazenly stare a man in the face. Immoderate laughter, wild gesticulation or running about the place is also *exceedingly unbecoming* in a female and may be taken as a token of a disturbed mind.

• Exercise dignity when sitting. Princess Charlotte reclines with her legs so outstretched that her drawers are exposed (such a liberal approach to the management of one's limbs is perhaps only to be outdone by the rather brutish Duchess of Bedford). One begins to abandon hopes that, at fifteen, her manners might not be fixed before she takes the throne.

• If your stock of beauty is small, do not intrude your ugliness upon the notice of unsuspecting bystanders, particularly if they are of a delicate constitution. Being unexpectedly confronted at close quarters by an unsightly stranger can provoke a serious attack of nerves.

• Crucially: prize your chastity. Female virtue, once lost, is lost forever.

PART TWO:

HINTS TO GENTLEMEN

GENTLEMEN are generally less attentive to personal appearance. However, just as a recruit into the Navy must be prepared mentally and sartorially for his journey, the first duty of a suitor is to equip himself properly for the trials of courtship. He is less likely to be thrown headfirst beneath a ship - and neither will he be provided with a daily ration of rum to steady his nerves - but the business of wooing is just as perilous for the uninitiated.

Knowing your Station

First, *consider your social position.* Quite apart from the revulsion that any sensible individual feels at the prospect of class *interbreeding,* pinning your hopes on someone more than one level your superior is an imprudent venture of humiliating proportions. Countless doomed suitors have ravished the hands of their betters and rendered both parties quite ridiculous. In all, as the following instructions reveal, a gentleman's conduct during courtship is in part determined by the consequence he derives from his rank.

You are:

1. A Prince of the Realm

It not being my place to impose rules on the conduct of the Royal Family, I shall confine myself to relating common practice. In short, royal blood appears to confer upon a person a licence to roam his hands about wherever he pleases, and to wander around the country committing outrages of propriety however he sees fit. In a lady, the Prince of Wales appears to prefer a buxomness of form and a face somewhat resembling a full moon; the Dukes of York and Clarence have a taste for profligate courtesans and actresses of extraordinary reproductive capabilities respectively. However, such women do not make royal wives.

DO: Appease your parents by marrying a regal cousin. If she is revolting, console yourself with the thought that your duty may be fulfilled with a single coital encounter.

DO NOT: Neglect the opportunity of taking mistresses. The disappointment of a quarrelsome or unattractive spouse may be atoned for in the embraces of a new wife each night.

2. A Titled Landowner, or Heir Thereto

The daughters of families boasting little fashion and no beauty should be disregarded entirely (note that your parents are likely to have arranged a match on your behalf, which may need to be negotiated).

DO: Choose your partner from one of the three or four hundred noble families of England (cousins often prove a convenient choice). English women are to be preferred.

DO NOT: Embroil yourself in dalliances with servant girls; they have a provoking tendency to conceive children and invariably expect you to pay for them.

3. A Younger Son in a Family of Nobility

It is customary for the younger sons of distinguished families to fall into one of the following professions:

a) Military officer

The military uniform has a fatal effect on the hearts of many impressionable females, regardless of the charms of the man wearing it. The world is currently in raptures over the exploits of a certain Richard Sharpe, a low-born soldier heavily engaged in seducing the desirable ladies of England and Spain. As he is, by all accounts, the illegitimate son of a prostitute - who has expended no energy whatsoever on correcting his deplorable Yorkshire accent - I can only attribute such success to the allure of his regimentals.

b) Clergyman

A respectable clergyman may select a partner from the middling ranks. It must be said, however, that such a course of action must only be attempted by those with strong spiritual inclinations - to those without, ladies preferring a religious man are apt to be considered the dullest wives ever destined to make domestic life insufferable.

DO: Improve your meagre financial prospects by joining the military or the clergy.

DO NOT: Forget that unless your elder brothers seem liable to suffer a premature death, you are of little use to your parents. As your mere existence is likely to be a burden, it is your duty to marry well.

3. From a Professional Family, of New Fortune

It is likely that your family money has been acquired through innovations in industry. By perfecting the polished exterior of a landed gentleman you may achieve a good match, particularly if the lady is rather more intrigued by your common roots than sickened by them.

DO: Invest in a good blue coat and suppress all outward signs of your innate coarseness.

DO NOT: Forget to keep considerable distance between polite society and your uncouth relatives, to prevent unfortunate social encounters. Settling them in a secure estate in Lancashire (or somewhere similarly remote) should suffice.

5. Skilled Tradesman, of No Fortune

Your inferior birth inhibits you from forming designs on ladies of quality. Do not attempt it. Direct your attentions at the daughters of neighbouring tradesmen – they are unlikely to be especially captivating in looks or in conversation but will be skilled in peeling vegetables, which is to be commended in a tradesman's wife.

DO: Impress her father with your craftsmanship by whittling him a chair or moulding him a new clay pipe.

DO NOT: Insist upon making fashionable ladies sick with your coarse professions of love. She will be entirely unable to detect anything commendable in your person, you may be sure.

6. A Manual Labourer

As most peasants do not take the care to learn to read, I do not feel bound to trouble myself on their account overmuch. They need only know that, wherever they are, they must be the lowest, and last.

DO: Choose your wife from among your own ranks. If a woman bemoans wallowing in dirt with the pigs, she is too refined for you.

DO NOT: Fret if you change your mind - it is common practice among the least polished societies of the world to take an unwanted wife to the local market or tavern with a halter around her neck, and sell her to the highest bidder.

There is only one species of *man* left to speak of, if he is deserving of such a title:

7. The Rake

A man with no more pressing employment than the seduction of impressionable females, who lives only to drink, play at cards and sport with women's feelings. Only when you have reformed your ways may you be instructed in the respectable arts of genuine courtship. Until then you are not permitted to continue deluding respectable women out of their senses, and into your bedchambers, with whatever wheedling devices it is you employ.

DO: Abandon the gaming-table and mend your profligate ways.

DO NOT: Even *begin* to contemplate fixing your attentions on my sister.

WHAT FEMALES WANT

With sundry reflections on how to appear desirable to them

HAVING identified the class of female to whom you may make your suit, we proceed to direction in appearing desirable to them. It is a peculiarity of the sex that most females expect - with no small degree of solemnity, I assure you - that we should be able to *read their minds.* Females delight in expressing the exact opposite of their feelings, sometimes from absence of mind, but usually in an attempt to elicit some proof of a companion's true character. Gentlemen, this treacherous terrain must be negotiated from the moment we take an interest in the opposite sex.

There are three basic masculine qualities that all women hope to discover in a suitor:

1. Unimaginable Wealth
2. Irresistible Good Looks
3. Exceptional Breeding

If you find, on looking into your affairs, that instead of being *very rich* you are in fact destined to be *very poor,* my counsel on the latter two points must be studied most diligently.

I: WEALTH

The possession of a fortune

Few women will refuse their heart when gold demands it, and there is no deficiency of character that cannot be greatly improved by the prospect of ten thousand pounds a year. The possession of a fortune - or failing that, at least a title - is the surest way to inspire the wildest of affections with the least effort.

A magnificent estate

A splendid property of impeccable taste will dispose even the most unyielding of hearts towards you. Ensure that your estate stirs admiration in every kind of temperament - invest in a library, a fishing pond, extensive grounds - and adorn the halls with endless flattering portraits (perhaps even a marble bust or two) of yourself looking impossibly noble and handsome.

Inform your housekeeper that visitors are permitted to tour the grounds in your absence (on the condition that they appear to be of respectable habits, and show no signs of suffering from communicable diseases).

The trappings of wealth

Female notice will inevitably be excited by a man with so much wealth that he is (almost) at a loss for disposing of it. A host of liveried servants, a glittering chaise and four and other trifling expenditures will all serve to give this impression. Now that philanthropy is grown fashionable, it may also be worthwhile to donate to the Foundling Hospital or a local fund for the destitute. Perceived generosity will persuade observers of your benevolence and will be particularly welcome in the eyes of prospective wives.

Impressive connections

Extensive patronage from noble kindred and affluent associates will secure an easy introduction into the most prestigious social and professional clubs – the more glamorous your circle, the more attractive you shall be.

II: ATTRACTIVENESS OF PERSON

However potent the advantage of great material assets, few men can afford to be utterly indifferent to their appearance. Even a rich young lord may find his advances rebuffed if he pays no heed to basic standards of hygiene. Certain physical features render a man infinitely more attractive to ladies, and I find myself very fortunate in my possession of them all. If you are not so happily endowed, there is little point in mourning and wondering over your own unseasonable ugliness - you must take action. The four most important characteristics to attend to are:

1. Height
2. Build
3. Odour
4. Sideburns

1. Be Tall. Great height has the double advantage of effortlessly asserting one's masculinity and enabling one to peer down at one's company with effective disdain. Napoleon's diminutive figure is a favourite joke in this country, but as he has managed to charm and discard Josephine - one of Europe's most fashionable women - I daresay he cannot be quite so small as they suppose. Nature alone can determine the loftiness of your stature, but improving your posture may lessen your shortcomings in this department. Failing this, invest in a monstrous tall hat.

2. *Improve Your Physique By Exercise*. Riding, swimming and shooting sculpt the physique into a vision of manly prowess. I have also found walking purposefully through the Derbyshire mist particularly beneficial (an auxiliary motive is that you expose yourself to the observation of passing females, who may inadvertently lose themselves in the contemplation of your perfections).

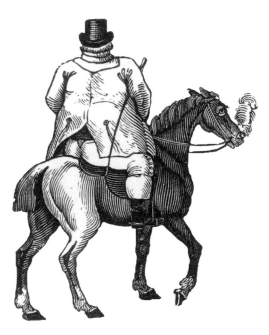

3. Pay Attention to Your Odour. While it is usually a promising sign if passing ladies routinely fall into swoons, it may be advisable to verify that they do so because their senses have been overwhelmed by your remarkable allure, and not the potency of your body odour. Our fathers were fond of over-using chemical scents and posies, but it is now the thing to bathe in water.

4. Cultivate Impressive Sideburns. A man's authority is often reflected in the arrangement and lustre of his facial hair. A bearded man is, obviously, a Wildman or a lunatic. The greased mustachios to be found lurking under the noses of men of the Continent are beginning to make their presence known in town, but I daresay the trend won't last long. On the contrary, a healthy pair of sideburns, resplendent in their wild luxuriant bushiness, will mark you out as an Englishman of mature understanding and original genius.

On Cosmetic Enhancement

The measures taken by men to artificially enhance their charms have a long if not exactly illustrious history (for the sake of those with delicate nerves, I shall abstain from mentioning the armoured codpieces so enthusiastically coveted by Henry VIII). Until recently men of all situations were defined by the size and state of their wig. The spindly of leg may stuff their stockings with horsehair for a well-rounded calf. There are whispers abroad that the Prince Regent wears a corset to control his bodily bulges (inspiring the impertinent to bestow upon him the title 'royal sausage'). If you must resort to such measures, it is of paramount importance that no-one should discover it.

On Dress

The upstart Beau Brummell, having gained renown for presuming to dictate what should or should not be fashionable, did express a keen interest in penning a few words on the subject for inclusion in this book. I refused his request on the ground that, whatever his influence, I am inclined to question most seriously the intellect of any man who devotes two hours each morning to the tying of his cravat. There is nothing more vexing than looking frightful when one particularly wishes to be seducing. To avoid such a calamity, invest in a well-cast looking-glass and pay the following small attentions to your dress:

- *Coats.* Ladies routinely fall into raptures at the sight of a man riding gallantly by on horseback in a dashing blue coat. Dark green, black and grey are also acceptable. These sober colours convey nobleness of mind, whereas lighter tones suggest levity of character.

- *Shirts.* Must be kept perfectly clean and white at all times. Apt to cling to the skin when wet.

- *Breeches.* Breeches and stockings should be worn at formal occasions, but longer trousers are now considered acceptable for everyday wear. Those clinging close to the thigh are curiously popular with females - buckskin breeches may be soaked and shrunk for a particularly snug fit.

- *Hats.* For outside wear. While we are now quite used to the sight, the towering silk top hat sent nearby ladies into fainting fits when it was first worn in London in 1797. By the usual laws of size eliciting admiration, you may still be sure of gaining the special notice of the ladies by obtaining the largest of all your acquaintance.

A foreigner of the name Ferdinand de Géramb has been parading around town sporting a perversely hairy monstrosity of a hat, adorned with tassles and heron feathers! Mercifully the fashion has not caught on - the ungracious manner in which they protrude into one's personal space renders this quite as much of a relief to sensible society as it should be to England's native heron population.

On the importance of a good tailor. There are few things more mortifying to the sensibilities than an ill-fitting suit of clothes. Added to the unsightly effect produced is the risk of loudly bursting one's waistcoat buttons, and the strings of one's pantaloons behind, at every deep sigh. Fortune dictates that there will be dead silence in the company, at the moment of the melancholy explosion.

On dandyism. While good taste and quality tailoring are essential, do not degrade yourself by falling into the effeminate class of dandy, whose heads are empty bulbous excresences used only as a podium upon which to display a ridiculous mass of hair. Sensible ladies are as unlikely to embrace a simpering fop to their bosom as a festering Cheapside beggar.

Further Reflections on Military Uniforms. Ladies are frequently to be observed wantonly throwing their handkerchiefs in the faces of officers as they pass by, or emitting a high-pitched tittering that increases in volume as they approach. Aside from the distinction of regimentals, the dress of an officer of the Royal Navy also excites general admiration. At a ball in 1804, Lady Hamilton once divulged - in something of a stupor, I might add - that Lord Nelson was originally induced to join the Navy, in part, by his father's hope that the attractive tricorn hat might disguise the unsightly shape of his head. Thus have cosmetic concerns altered the whole course of British history.

On Hair

The following article, recently published in a London journal, offers some insight into the signals that may be given out by the arrangement of one's hair.

The language of hair

- The morose and the blunt man, the drunkard and the hard-fisted mechanic, have their hair *unkempt, unclean, and sticking out* in most admired disorder.

- *Baldness* is ordinarily the sign of an active mind, unless the man brushes his hair forward, which is a vulgar affectation; or still worse, wears a wig, in which case he must be set down as an antiquated fool.

- *Stiff hair* is a sign of obstinate character.

- A *curly head* is almost uniformly indicative of wit and a love of pleasure.

- *Prematurely grey hair* is a sign either of profound anxiety or secret nocturnal dissipation.

- *Copious unclean locks,* which grease the collar and shoulders, belong to none but pretended philosophers, incomprehensible critics, inferior artists and journeymen tailors.

- *Beards, moustachios or a single, long eyebrow* are a mark either of foreign birth, unnatural inclinations, or a regrettable mixture of the two.

III: GOOD BREEDING

No matter how carefully a man grooms and prinks, it does not always follow that he will devote equal attention to his comportment. Any youth of nineteen will suffer the horror of contriving how to adjust one's legs and arms in a drawing room without eliciting numerous condolences on the spasmodic tortures under which he seems to be labouring; no matter how exceptional his lineage.

While those of noble blood have a distinct natural advantage, an air of sophistication can be cultivated. Contrary to popular assumption, however, good breeding does not equate to universal affability, and manners should be calculated less to *please* than to *overawe*.

One must master five skills, to be exercised at all public occasions:

- An air of aloof indifference

- Manly command of the room

- Silent mastery of the ballroom

- Learning to speak properly, but exercising that ability as little as possible

- No unnecessary smiling

Thus:

Arrive fashionably late. You shall receive a more grateful welcome, and will be rendered all the more impressively handsome by candle-light. Make a grand entrance but refuse to seek introductions, instead glowering silently around the room. Let your behaviour be sober, stand tall and convey general disdain by means of vaguely intimidating body language. Revealing nothing of your innermost thoughts - except perhaps to pass comment on the failings of others - will impress upon the company your superiority of mind, and encourage them to be more solicitous of gaining your approval.

Position yourself so as to command general attention, and adopt a manly and confident posture.

Do not drink so much as to make you see double, lisp your words, stagger around the room or fall to sleep. If insufferable acquaintances threaten to approach, deter their advances by ignoring them entirely or pacing about the room, observing always to keep your body upright and even. There is always the hope that the company will stand in such awe that they shall not even venture to speak to you at all.

Dancing, however tedious the exercise, is a necessary skill for a modern gentleman and affords an opportunity for exhibiting one's noble bearing. To effectively overwhelm the assembled throng, refuse to dance for as long as possible, and loudly bemoan how much you abhor the whole blasted business. The moment you deign to choose a partner, all eyes will be drawn to you (consult chapter IV for more detailed discussion of dancing as a means of impressing the lady).

Rational conversation may be rarely detected in lesser society, and even in the highest circles is frustrated by the lamentable vogue for voicing all manner of nonsense merely for the sake of drawing all ears to one's lips (the tendency of females to wear revealing gowns for the sake of drawing all eyes to their bosom is similarly abhorrent). Most importantly: acquaint yourself with the rudiments of civilised conversation, avoid common proverbs and perfect your pronunciation.

Some Hints On Pronunciation

Common errors committed by the ill-educated:

Busy - Bizzy
Chaise - Shaze
Conscience - Conshunce
Daughter - Dawter
Physician - Fizzishun
&c &c.

Business - Biznes
Circl - Surcle
Cupboard - Cubbard
Housewife - Huzzif
Toilet - Twalet, or Twilight

Similarly, if you find yourself afflicted by a villainous cold in the head, do not disgust yourself and your company with lusty blowing of the nose during conversation, and incorrectly pronouncing *M* like *B* and *N* like *D*, &c.

Smiling is generally uncalled for. Affectations of pleasure will encourage people to believe that their company is not only tolerated but is actually *agreeable*, and subsequently they shall continue to annoy you with it. Inane grinning denotes a vacuity of mind, whereas *intense staring* conveys an alluring air of intelligence and mystery.

IF YOUR CHARMS ARE LIMITED

IDENTIFY your natural attractions, perfect them and display them to their best advantage. If you cannot count wealth, dashing looks and good breeding among your merits, do not throw yourself into raptures of despair. Emphasise your positive attributes. In general, men lacking refinement can compensate with a well-groomed coiffure and a glittering chaise and four. Those without wealth must be pleasing in every other way.

Some achieve remarkable success with ladies despite being frightful ogres. The phenomenon is common among politicians. Though his appearance was not calculated to recommend him in anyone's eyes, the radical John Wilkes repeatedly proved that he could "get the better of any man, however good-looking, in the graces of any lady" given the start of fifteen minutes. In his case, boorish wit apparently precluded the necessity for a handsome face.

IF YOU HAVE NO CHARM
WHATSOEVER

HOW may a man enjoying neither fame, name nor good looks hope to engage a lady's affections? Fix your hopes on a generally unadmired female. Attend the same entertainments. Once your unfortunate face has become a familiar (perhaps even tolerable) sight, you may begin to move in the same social circles and seek an introduction. Grateful for your attentions, she may be disposed to encourage them despite your obvious defects. If she is not immediately obliging you may always hope that as her own prospects run into further decline - perhaps through ageing or the loss of her chastity - she may begin to view you with more interest.

If you cannot charm a woman of sense, you may as well set up something that fools will admire. Silly women are seduced by all manner of unspeakable buffoonery and idle jest: hard drinking, the quantity of snuff a man can force up his nostrils, gymnastic tricks while riding, &c. I have known one acquaintance utterly beguiled by the 'great joke' of her male companion dressing himself in one of her gowns! Of course, I should never recommend such ridiculous females to the notice of respectable men, but fellows devoid of all merit must content themselves with similarly preposterous wives.

CHAPTER III

Selecting a Wife

IT highly behoves persons of all ranks seriously to consider the qualifications of those upon whom they will settle their affections. The novelty of choice - and freedom from the whims of our parents - brings with it no small degree of consternation.

Regrettably, many older persons continue to cherish their antiquated matchmaking schemes with unyielding obstinacy. My aunt, Lady Catherine, is excessively fond of informing my female acquaintances that I shall soon be united with her own daughter. This shall, no doubt, become something of a bore when I am inclined to take a wife. I do not quibble that Miss de Bourgh has many qualities to recommend her - I daresay her various medical complaints should render her a perfectly fascinating companion for a physician, or student of science. I wish her, and her mother, every good fortune in their matrimonial plans, but they shall never tempt me.

Nevertheless, the pleasantness of a person's company does not always evince its propriety, and one must also avoid such unsuitable infatuation as will inevitably cloud the judgment of even rational men. The following chapter - primarily addressed to the gentleman reader, as a lady is rarely allowed to exercise the power of choice - reveals the most effective methods of identifying a potential partner, and ensuring that she is adequately qualified for the post.

ON CONQUERING
INFATUATION

IMPRESSIONABLE young men have a dreadful propensity for believing themselves to be dying for a new lady's hand every few weeks. The emotional struggle is unspeakably painful to the sufferer, but it is common custom for him to muster the energy to speak of nothing else, punctuated with heavy sighing and the composition of appalling sonnets in admiration of his lady's eyebrow, front tooth, or some such nonsense.

In plain words, there should be no 'falling in love', except with suitable persons. For the benefit of all parties inappropriate passions must be conquered, and this can only be achieved with firmness of mind and the exercise of solid reason. As soon as you conceive a passion – particularly if the object is an extraordinary beauty – take the time to examine at leisure whether she has not some concealed deformity. Whereas some faults may be plainly seen, others are revealed only after thorough investigation.

Inquiries must be made into her character, reputation, situation and the circumstances of her family. If the lady is a widow, you may even find yourself in the happy position of discovering how she conducts herself as a wife (ensure, of course, that her late husband was not killed in mysterious or otherwise scandalous circumstances).

As a step towards conversing with her yourself, secretly attend to her conversation with others. If you discover that she is intellectually unsound or indifferent to normal standards of decorum, any esteem formerly felt may be quite easily suppressed. Similarly, if you are disgusted by her inferior connections, questionable history or penchant for mindless romantic novels, the brightness of that object you began to hold in tender regard will grow dim and disappear. If, however, you remain satisfied with her person, you are permitted to form designs upon her.

IS SHE QUALIFIED TO BE YOUR WIFE?

THERE are many aspects to be considered in the selection of a partner. Perfection is not frequently to be met with, but a distinguished personage must examine the niceties of a lady's conduct and habits before forming a design upon her. Mr Beau Brummell, for example, quite understandably broke off an engagement with a lady because he saw her eat cabbage. Of course, those who cannot afford to be so fastidious should content themselves with a female whose amiable qualities are sufficiently predominant to stamp her general character. In your preliminary inquiries, satisfy yourself on the following points. Is the lady:

1. Of the appropriate social status?

This may be settled by consulting the preceding chapter and your common sense. It would be folly to introduce an unpolished country maid - all mud and uncouth language - to polite society and expect the matter to go off well. By the same token, a lowly farmer cannot suppose that a woman raised in silk will relinquish her finery and cavort with the pigs in his stable.

Certainly [ ]   Indubitably not [ ]

2. Of good stock?

Careful inquiry into her father's profession and social standing is imperative. Pedigree is an important consideration - you are binding yourself to the lady's family for the duration of your life. Would any man of sense attach himself to a father unable to hold his brandy, a mother unable to hold her tongue and sisters unable to hold on to their petticoats? Some even settle on prospective in-laws before setting their aim at one of the daughters. I do not think it ill-judged to attach yourself to a family with professional concerns closely tied to your own: if you are pursuing a career in law, choose the daughter of a local magistrate; if your heart is set on the selling of vegetables, court the daughter of a green-grocer (note: if your interest is *entirely* mercenary, you may do well to attach yourself to the ugliest of his female relatives - there will be no limit to his gratitude).

Abandon all thought of a lady whose true parentage is in question. It will be discovered too late that, far from being the darling orphan of a mysterious aristocrat, your beloved is in fact the fruit of an illegitimate liaison between a travelling basket-seller and a bar-maid. This dreadful inheritance will be a curse to your own offspring, who will enter this world with an evil countenance and depart it on the end of a rope. Such an association would be most degrading for your respectable parents.

Certainly ☐   Indubitably not ☐

3. Admired by other gentlemen?

Observe the manner in which other gentlemen address the lady and how widely she is generally esteemed. Even if her faults are not immediately forthcoming, there is little reason to waste time giving consequence to those who are slighted by other men – there is clearly some lurking deficiency.

Certainly ☐   Indubitably not ☐

4. Fortunate in her share of beauty?

A fine-looking wife will secure the envy of your associates and is usually advantageous in the begetting of handsome children. However, a beauty trusting only to her outward charms commonly proves to be a cross prig and, rather than offer consolation, the neighbourhood will reward your conceit by treating the miserable match as a capital joke. Beauties are in the habit of taking themselves for little goddesses, but choose a lady who pays some attention to her appearance, for a sloven in dress is careless in everything.

Certainly ☐   Indubitably not ☐

5. Blessed with appropriate sharpness of mind?

A woman possessed of natural common sense is a rarity indeed; even rarer is the intelligent woman who will properly submit to the direction of a stupid husband. For this reason, the intellectual properties of a man ought never to be obviously inferior to those of his wife.

Certainly ☐   Indubitably not ☐

6. Skilled in pecuniary matters?

A woman must have a first-class understanding of domestic matters. Many respectable men have been ruined by extravagant wives - my father's steward unhappily fell to this unenviable fate - and if she entertains herself by reading silly novels, dressing in ribbons and gadding about shops (the general symptoms of being a complete simpleton) then her husband must bid his peaceful existence farewell.

Certainly ☐   Indubitably not ☐

7. Accomplished?

If you hope to impress polite society with your choice of wife, she must exhibit adequate talent for music, dancing, embroidery and the arts. She will not be generally esteemed if she cannot display excellence in at least one, or proficiency in all, of these genteel accomplishments. If you aim only at women of lower orders, it is rather more important for them to cultivate skills in cooking, cleaning, boiling the kettle, bearing sons, &c.

Certainly ☐   Indubitably not ☐

8. Of unimpeachable moral character?

Always avoid her in whom love of pleasure appears a predominant passion. I shall not dwell on the importance of chastity, lest the mere mention stirs impure thoughts in the mind of my reader. Nevertheless, a woman easily won should not be trusted with the momentous charge of providing you with legitimate offspring.

Certainly ☐   Indubitably not ☐

9. Conscious of her rightful place?

Better to have no wife at all than to have to tolerate an ungovernable one.

Certainly ☐   Indubitably not ☐

10. *Of a temperament that will harmonise with your own?*

If you are yourself hasty and passionate, seek one who is of a meek disposition; if you are meek, I would recommend a person of vivacity. Whatever your character, ensure that she is willing to serve you.

Certainly  Indubitably not

11. *A suitable age?*

It is quite common to enter into matrimony in one's twenties. If you hope for a large family, select a wife in her late teens - by keeping her in a constant state of pregnancy you could feasibly achieve a brood of twenty or so (although I warn you that such exertions have left our Queen frail and our King quite mad in their dotage). If she has seen more than thirty summers she is likely to be of little use in this regard.

A significant difference in age usually indicates a match based on material concerns. Married last week in Lambton, after a tedious courtship of three days, were Mr James Watts, a farmer aged 19, and Mary Astin, a widow of 80 years in possession of no inconsiderable wealth (following the demise of her third husband a fortnight past). The bridegroom's face was quite the picture of horror when his new wife - whom he thought might soon be led to her grave - proceeded to dance several reels at the wedding with as much agility as a girl of twenty. Such is the unhappy lot of the fortune hunter.

Certainly ☐ Indubitably not ☐

If you answered 'certainly' to every question, the lady is in every respect qualified for the situation. If this was beyond your power, I advise you to reconsider your choice.

A suitable wife for a gentleman   *An unsuitable wife for a gentleman*

IDENTIFYING SINGLE FEMALES

IT is highly improper to pay amorous compliments to a lady whose hand is already spoken for. Such careless wooing will lead, at best, to an awkward rebuff or, at worst, to a potentially fatal encounter with her husband. Fortunately, there are ways of distinguishing between females who are already attached, and those who are not. First, interrogate your mutual acquaintances (this has the secondary benefit of requiring you to expend no more energy than it takes to utter a handful of words). If the lady is entirely unknown, examine her demeanour. With their matrimonial mission accomplished, those already engaged exude a certain species of confidence rarely exhibited by single ladies in all the agonies of an uncertain future. As such, the former are often the most likely to "take a chirruping-glass" (to use a common phrase) with undue alacrity. Symptoms of this unfeminine excess are glazed expressions, an air of self-satisfaction and a tendency to speak loudly and boldly on the amorous affairs of others. Conversely, an unattached female is likely to be in the company of other ladies, dressed with great care and rather more timid when approached by a gentleman.

Apparently hoping to be of service to prospective suitors, the fair sex have also devised covert signals by which we may ascertain their marital status without a word passing their lips. As a consequence, countless generations of men have been forced to master unspoken languages that are ten times as difficult to interpret as simple conversation, and as changeable as a Drury Lane actress.

A short time ago a public journal valiantly offered the following translation of how a female may broadcast her marital status by the use of her jewellery:

"When a lady is *not engaged,* she wears a hoop or diamond on the first finger; if *engaged* on the second finger; if *married,* on the third; and on the fourth, if she intends to *die a maiden.*"

I daresay this trend will last a month before the ladies see fit to amuse themselves by contriving a new system based on the tilt of their bonnets or the number of ribbons in their hair. It is enough to drive a rational man to distraction.

WHAT MAY BE
REVEALED BY THE
STATE OF HER FACE

THE science of determining a person's disposition by their hair, eyes, nose, &c, has a long history. It is supposed that, by their continual exercise, the passions actually stamp certain characteristics onto the body. By this means alone some dubious persons claim to be able to read the face as easily as a book, differentiating between rogues, honest men, wise folk and simpletons. It is a favourite trick of travelling vagabonds, but you will find the topic often discussed by fashionable parties, enthusiasm for it having recently been revived by a superstitious Swiss poet of the name Lavater. The following notes from a pocket guide recently published reveal some of the basic principles.

Notes on Physiognomy,
by a doctor of distinction.

Most of the below observations will hold generally true in either sex.

Eyes

Eyes look a-squint - deceitful disposition of mind
Rolling, wandering eye - lustful and cunning
Grey - quick temper, love of novelty
Hazel - shrewd, such as take pleasure in intercourse with friends
Blue - good judge of character
Drooping eyelids - of cunning, secretive habits

Nose

Long and great nose - lover of the fair sex, and well accoutered for the purpose
Short and flat - the reverse
Turned up at the point - rich in talents, exceedingly jealous
Very small, with an improper upper lip - lack of discretion
Thick, bulbous ends - insensitive and swinish
Red nose and cheeks - frequently intoxicated

Mouth

Wide mouth and full cheeks - cross person fit for little business, given to folly

Large disproportion between upper and lower lips - sign of stupidity

Sharply delineated, thin lips - easily intimidated and fearful

Absence of teeth - lack of attention to basic hygiene

Head & Hair

Strong and red - lustful and dissipated

Blond - a noble soul

Black - boldness and love of adventure

Brown - hot head and good temper

Other

Finely-arched forehead of great magnitude - betokening royal dignity and maturity

The fewer hollows in the forehead - the more destitute of ideas

Square ears - sublimity of soul

Puffed cheeks, freckles in the face - a character of worthless insignificance

Mole upon the buttocks - of a pliant and affable temper

While some derive entertainment from such fanciful notions, I would not advise selecting a partner purely from her doe-like demeanour, or from the protrusion of his chin. One mulish man of my acquaintance attached himself to a particularly disagreeable woman simply because he believed the strong lines on her hand denoted 'easy and prodigious child-bearing'. Fifteen years and one sickly babe later, I fear he rather regrets the unusual store he set by her exceptionally wrinkled fingers – which she only ever puts to work on opening the gin bottle.

ON THE DECEPTIONS OF BEAUTIFUL WOMEN

ONE must always be on one's guard against the most infernal set of miscreants that ever lived - ladies who make sport, even a profession, of bewitching men out of their fortunes. The most successful of these creatures are mindful of their extraordinary personal charms, falling into one of two categories:

- an artful female seeking to empty a man's purse by marriage

- an immoral female seeking to empty a man's purse without marriage

If a female appears to show interest in you, examine her carefully. Beneath the angelic exterior may lurk a charlatan, a prostitute or - worst of all - an advocate of liberal politics.

The Artful Female

Some ladies practise any deception at their disposal to secure an affluent husband. Fortune-hunting parents delivered of unusually attractive daughters often raise them to be cunning, teaching them to disguise not only their faults but also their true dispositions under the appearance of insinuating sweetness.

Each year hundreds of unsuspecting gentlemen are ensnared in such a trap. Almost as soon as the vows are taken the lady's engaging good humour and pretended affection are swept away by an all-consuming desire to arrange balls, trips to Bath and other schemes for disposing of your fortune. No matter how extensive your income, they will always exceed it.

The Immoral Female

As the sailor must beware the lures of sirens, so the respectable Englishman must spurn the advances of women of loose virtue. The most dangerous class of these females masquerade as gentlewomen and parade about the pleasure gardens, theatres and taverns with as much affected politeness as a high-born duchess, only revealing what they are about when they see fit to reveal the price attached to their company. Be attentive to the fact that whatever arrangement is reached, they are likely to throw an unwelcome medical complaint into the bargain.

Hints towards Recognising a Harlot

For the sake of your manhood and your good name, these signs of lost virtue should be committed to memory:

1. Your acquaintance was formed with no proper introduction

2. She wears paint on her face

3. She is frequently to be found in a state of inebriation

4. She promises to make an alarmingly enthusiastic bedfellow

5. She has a background in the theatre or other form of public entertainment

6. She wears pearls or diamonds early in the morning

7. Other men address her with impertinent familiarity, and she does not swoon with mortification

8. She speaks often of her 'sisters' but is disinclined to introduce you to her family or to inform you of their residence

9. You often find her skulking about dark alleyways

10. You discover her in bed with another man

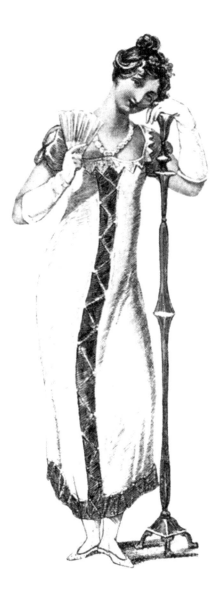

IS THE LADY ALL SHE SEEMS?

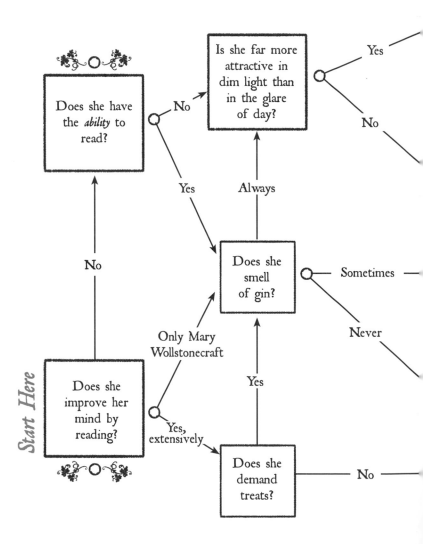

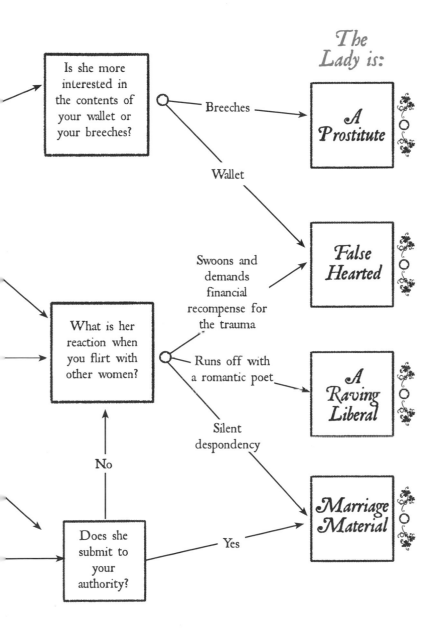

Marriage Material: Congratulations. This female understands the inferior position of her sex, and appears perfectly suitable to be courted by a sensible man.

Raving Liberal: I regret to inform you that your lady appears to entertain liberal ideas that will undoubtedly be your ruin. Possibly deranged.

False Hearted: She may be a fortune-hunter, a *coquette*, or simply encouraging your attentions for sport. She is likely to continue the charade until you are married, after which time she will prove to be an utter disappointment and have no misgivings about making you a cuckold.

Prostitute: Whether courtesan or a common harlot, your lady is clearly of loose virtue and will under no circumstances make a suitable spouse.

N.B. It is perfectly possible for a woman to be interested in both your breeches and your wallet – such a one may be called a false-hearted prostitute.

LOCATING ELIGIBLE FEMALES

In Town & Country

ARMED with this knowledge about identifying a suitable female, you are now permitted to sally forth into the public arena to select her.

Men of *great* standing, such as myself, need not expend much effort on this exercise - eligible females will be eager to seek out your company. Whenever you intend to grace a neighbourhood with your presence, simply let it be known that a bachelor of a remarkable fortune is soon to be among them. The locals will instantly feel compelled to fashion their daughters into a semblance of politeness, hopefully sparing you the horror of rustic manners in all their crudeness. Interested families with varying pretensions to elegance will conspire to annoy you, but mastery of the precepts found in chapter II will enable you to spot the riff-raff, and ignore them accordingly.

Some gentlemen are in the habit of making excursions with the particular intention of examining the local females and contemplating the possibility of making one his wife. If you meditate such a scheme, consider the gentility of your destination and amend your expectations to suit.

Thus:

1. *When visiting town,* take care to fall into the correct circles. In public places it is quite easy to find oneself suddenly lost amidst a fry of urban wretches, who shoal from all the unheard-of holes of the city and suburbs, apparently with little more pressing intent than that of revolting their betters.

2. Persons who haunt coastal resorts such as *Brighton* and *Ramsgate* are to be regarded with strict suspicion. Proximity to the seaside incites even sensible persons to loose behaviour.

3. *Bath* is generally insufferable on account of being populated almost solely by silly girls and the sick.

4. In general, one has not great hopes from *Birmingham.*

5. On *visiting the country* be prepared to tolerate much less varied, and usually rather uncivilised, society.

6. The *northern provinces of England* are generally considered wild and uncouth, as are the majority of its females.

7. Similarly, *ladies of foreign birth* tend to exhibit a distasteful lack of feminine reserve, and occasionally fail to observe basic standards of hygiene.

Hints for the fashionable

In town, a gentleman is routinely condemned to murder his evenings at an interminable succession of balls, pleasure gardens, theatres and masquerades. The only soothing balm to such tedious sacrifices of time, health and money is perhaps the opportunity for meeting persons of the opposite sex. The most splendid sort of property, and the most refined society, is to be found in the west, around Grosvenor Square. Avoid the eastern quarters, which - being populated by persons unaccountably begrimed by a mysterious sort of filth - are no place for those with pretensions to respectability.

In the country, society is rather more confined and opportunities for the sort of merriment that many consider instrumental in matters of love are not so easily met with. There may be some occasion for dancing, if you have a taste for such things, at which the local livestock will voluntarily expose their rustic idea of refinement. Such a setting will at least heighten your own superior qualities and render you even more devastatingly attractive.

Hints for the unfashionable

Those obliged to *work* for a living should take advantage of this opportunity to identify prospective partners. If your master or colleagues are of respectable stock, ingratiate yourself with them in the hope that they are looking to dispose of an unattached female relation.

The lower classes – who are often to be found swarming the streets, in savage jollity, after a bull-baiting, a boxing match, an execution, &c – also use such public entertainments to meet with members of the fair sex. Some reckless tavern proprietors and landowners also arrange public hop feasts and dances, offering the local rustics a crude imitation of the fashionable ball.

ADVERTISING FOR
A WIFE

IT is a testament to the abiding obsession with matrimony, that for as long as newspapers have been in circulation, men have submitted advertisements boldly reading 'WANTED: A WIFE'. It is now common for both sexes to make such announcements - just as if they were looking for a chambermaid or a stud-horse - and encourage applications for the post. I daresay one could contrive no surer way of exposing private matters to public derision. Individuals deriving benefit from consulting personal advertisements are likely to be those:

- With no other means of making acquaintance
- Past the bloom of youth
- Rendered dumb by timidity
- With little else to recommend them

Those of potent sensibility call such a courtship soulless, and those who derive comfort from convention consider this brazen familiarity with strangers to be foolish and undignified. Upon reading a particularly pert notice in *The Times* last month, Lady Catherine was so appalled that she was compelled to call immediately for the smelling salts - it took a full day to restore her composure.

Nevertheless, the method may be advantageous to those unblessed with the happy talent of conversing easily with strangers, and those who have too many demands on their time. One resounding qualification in its favour is that it requires minimal effort.

If you insist on making your amorous overtures in this manner, all responses must be regarded with the necessary suspicion. The whole business is a capital joke to the frivolous, who derive immense pleasure from inserting false advertisements and making sport of those who answer. Spending whole days gadding about coffeehouses in fits over the success of their pranks, they exhibit no reservations about making public the identities of their victims. Others persist further in the deception, as an elderly gentleman of Holborn discovered last week – having hurried to meet his enchanting correspondent in person, he was met instead by a mob of school-boys poised to pelt him with stones.

Set down, with brevity:

- The extent of your fortune
- Your other merits (eg. respectable profession, pleasing countenance)
- Required attributes in a partner (eg. appearance, disposition, income and, crucially, sex – neglecting this final point could lead to a most awkward encounter)
- Simple instructions for commencing the correspondence

Avoid:

- Long, rambling epistles
- Feeble attempts at flattery
- Complicated and fanciful modes of seeking an introduction
- Asking a lady to disclose her age

The following advert recently inserted in a local newspaper may be taken as an example of a strong suit.

TO THE LADIES.

A Gentleman wants a wife: she must be beautiful, sensible, polite, and displaying no such levity of behaviour as inevitably renders a beauteous face contemptible to the discerning part of the world. She must be humane and charitable, and of a respectable family. The advertiser is 25 years of age, immediate heir to a title, tall, and is made to believe very handsome.

All responses (post paid) to No. 45, Strand, London.

The regular advertisements of the late eccentric Sir John Dineley, Bt, demonstrate how *not* to go about the exercise. Rendering himself conspicuous by his dirty silk stockings and rapturous professions of servitude to any lady who would tolerate his company, he was a familiar personage around Windsor, until his demise three years past. To secure a young wife was the whole business of this elderly man's existence, but despite his promises of eleven thousand pounds, he succeeded only in repulsing all he addressed.

How happy will a Lady be,
To have a little Baronet, to dandle on her Knee

One of his more lucid advertisements ran thus:

FOR A WIFE.

Any Marriageable Lady with 300l. under the age of 21, or with 500l above that age, and who will convince me of her esteem, with her own hand writing in answer to this, and glory in her public affection, I, SIR JOHN DINELEY, Baronet, will settle Eleven Thousand Pounds a Year upon her, and other Estates she may bring with her; and will ever study to increase her happiness, and indulge her LADYSHIP to the highest degree in my power; and I will get her One Thousand Pounds a Year more by my well known Practice of Physick, if required.

I shall impatiently wait to see your signal with your second finger on your left hand: With it make a snug scratch between your eyes, before you pass by me, on the Terrace, or elsewhere, to denote your intention, to meet me in the Alcove near my house in WINDSOR CASTLE, when the clock strikes one; where you may find me every dry day. If you are alone, I shall hope to see you instantly move towards the Alcove. I shall introduce the subject by asking you if you can tell me how the Ladies approve of the enterprizing and remarkable Printed Marriage Offer, that SIR JOHN DINELEY has made them.

Yours, &c, Sir John.

CHAPTER IV

Winning her Affections

AND so we proceed to the most delicate phase of the whole business: securing the lady's affections. Once a suitable female has been selected, you may begin to form serious designs in wooing her. Being more than commonly anxious to please, many lovers naturally suspect that every power of pleasing will suddenly fail them. For the frail of heart the very notion may be intimidating, but do not despair - after all, Lord Nelson suffered from seasickness for his entire life, yet he is now hailed as the most accomplished naval hero in British history.

If you have adhered to the advice laid down thus far, you will have already gained the lady's notice, and probably her admiration - all that remains is to enchant her with your manly perfections. Regrettably, in order to do so, one must undergo all manner of irritating exercises and tests of character. Your inquiries into her temperament should afford some hints as to the best course of action: ladies inclined to seriousness will be impressed by philosophical discourse, but the heart of a simple milkmaid may be won by a lover's ballad and a wild flower.

In courtship, modesty is required in a woman and boldness in a man. In the following chapter I reveal the most expeditious means of engaging a person's heart through your behaviour, countenance, conversation and compliments. For the ladies I offer hints on properly receiving a man's addresses, and distinguishing between the earnest and the dishonourable.

A VERY ENGLISH ATTACK

IN times of war such as these, Englishmen pride themselves on their singularly bold and effectual skills in engagement with the enemy. Courtship may be viewed in quite the same way (although on no account are you to manhandle a female as you would an armed Frenchman).

In truth, the romantic rituals of our foreign cousins are often as inscrutable as their culinary preferences. The Italians - self-proclaimed experts in matters of love - are seldom favoured in this country on account of their offensively greased hair and fondness for walking about half-dressed. In France, before the unfortunate Revolution threw the nation into disarray, it was the fashion to simply insist upon a lady's hand, supporting the suit with lascivious language and vulgar gesticulation. A fanciful custom in Lapland requires a suitor to creep towards the house of his beloved cloaked in a wolf-skin and present her parents with a bottle of brandy.

The German mode of courtship is largely concerned with the giving and receiving of prized sausages. They also avail themselves of any excuse to engage in that most riotous and indecent of dances, the waltz, under which auspices a gentleman actually clasps his arm around an unknown lady's waist! Thankfully, in this country all respectable persons would frown most seriously on such behaviour and the unmentionable lusts it must excite.

The Spanish exhibit two unusual perversions in their treatment of the female sex. First, the ladies are revered to an extraordinary extent. It is considered improper to express any discontent with their conduct and if a lady fancies a jewel, her male companion is obliged to buy it (the women, unsurprisingly, are very much given to such whims). Second, many married noblewomen expect to be 'courted' by other consorts, who must beg to be admitted to her circle of admirers. And all with the consent of their husbands! Clearly the climate of that country has had a catastrophic effect on the intellect of its male inhabitants.

The English style of courtship is in all respects superior. By all means feel things deeply, but refrain from making your sentiments publicly known, unless it is absolutely necessary. Do not overwhelm the lady with too direct an attack, nor prostrate yourself before her with unmanly sentimentality. Such unreasonable females as will only value a courtship based on absurd flatteries and fripperies are not worth a regret. Quiet attentions, formally bestowed, will be more than sufficient.

BETTING BOOKS

KEEP in mind that the romantic intentions of any illustrious personage will not be kept under the cloak of secrecy for long, even if he is a master of discretion. All such affairs are mere sport to observers, and the rumoured schemes and misadventures of all players will eventually reach the betting books of gentlemen's clubs such as White's, Brooks's and the Cocoa-Tree Club. In certain circles gentlemen will abuse any opportunity of gambling, and often take the liberty of speculating on the amorous affairs of their fellows. Examples run thus:

- *Mr Howard bets Mr Raikes ten guineas that either Lord T or Lord Pomfret will marry Miss Long. — December 1, 1810. [Howard paid.]*

- *Mr Thorpe bets Mr Elliot a pony that a certain Miss Dashwood will succumb to the charms of Mr Willoughby before nine months this day. — April 19, 1812.*

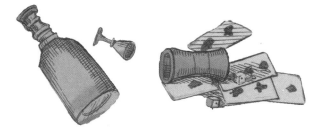

For a distinguished gentleman escape is virtually impossible. I am informed that the following bet registered last year at White's concerns myself and Miss Bingley:

- *Lord Alvanley bets Mr Talbot a hundred guineas that a certain person understood between them does not marry a certain lady understood between them in eighteen months from this day.* — *January 5, 1811.*

I console myself that, as my behaviour is at all times impeccable, my reputation is not injured by such idle conjecture. The insufferable Lord Alvanley is renowned for taking every opportunity to gamble; he has squandered fortunes laying wagers on the relative speed of raindrops down a windowpane, and the untimely deaths of his friends. Depriving the man of a hundred guineas would almost persuade me to attach myself to Miss Bingley, if only her character did not seem so inalterably calculated to irritate me.

SECURING AN INTRODUCTION

THE first proof of lowness is seen at once in undue familiarity, and if a particular lady deserves to have your perfections brought to her notice you must seek a proper introduction. Observing these codes of conduct distinguishes the refined from the offal of the human species, and imitating the latter by flitting around intruding yourself upon utter strangers will not do.

At public and private events one must never abandon proper etiquette in any respect. Many of my acquaintance have fallen foul of the machinations of insolent journalists, who are much given to secretly attending to one's conversations. Their deserved reputation for hard drinking rarely works to one's advantage, and you may find that an inclination vaguely expressed at an evening ball is depicted as a lewd proposal in the morning papers.

The gentleman should always be introduced to the lady. If possible, discover a mutual acquaintance capable of presenting you to the chosen one with an adequate sense of gravity and occasion. If her conversation reveals her to be utterly uninteresting or uncivilised, it is better to extricate yourself from the situation immediately rather than encouraging the forlorn hopes that she will have inevitably begun to nurture in her breast. A simple bow and sharp departure will suffice, and you may then justifiably proceed to ignore her for the rest of the evening. If she is of lower standing she will almost certainly have been frightened by your contempt; if she is your better, she will not risk the indignity of being further slighted by you.

SECURING HER AFFECTIONS

IF she does not wholly repulse you upon initial acquaintance, it now remains only to gain her esteem. If skilfully executed this can be achieved quite in the same way as training a dog to obedience, or breaking in a wild horse:

- Overawe her with your masterful authority
- Become familiar to her
- Show some *small* symptoms of gentleness or regard
- Ignore her and/or walk away

Nine times out of ten the lady's heart will go with you.

Having liberally treated of point a) I shall advance immediately to point b). Not all men inspire women to run distracted with effusions of love upon first acquaintance. The timid retreat to a darkened corner, skulk about and nurse futile hopes that their pitiful first impression was sufficient to amaze her. To these men I say, most assuredly, *it was not*. In order to cultivate a liking sort of love it is necessary to ensure that thoughts of you fill her head, so that they may promptly proceed to conquer her heart. Whether her early opinions of you are based in desire, curiosity or even dislike, is not of much consequence.

When out and about, make it your business to discover her regular or preferred retreats, *and lurk there indiscriminately*. Walk with manly purpose before her window, encounter her by 'chance' in a pretty glade or woodland, and appear to her rescue when she is poised on the brink of muddying her skirts in a puddle. When you have occasion to converse, insist on escorting her to her destination with such a degree of speed and solemn expedience as cannot fail to impress.

At social events, *thrust yourself into her line of vision* as often as possible. There is a delicate balance to strike; you should expect to fluster her a little, but do not alarm her so much as to cause a swoon or an unbecoming attack of nerves.

Engage her interest by fleeting displays of gentleness. Before you present yourself, perfect a noble expression and adopt it at all times (study your features in a looking glass, if you must). When you feel her gaze fall upon you do not acknowledge it, but allow a momentary impression of private wistfulness and swiftly follow it with a long episode of grave contemplation. By this means she may become intrigued by your inner torment without being disgusted by an unmanly failure to control it. If it is absolutely necessary you are permitted on occasion to offer some small token of regard, such as an invitation to dance or a direct and intent stare when she plays an instrument in public. The lady is likely to be so grateful for your attentions that she will instantly be more disposed to fall in love with you.

Once the notion of your favour has been planted in her head and her interest has been engaged, it is vital that you become again a model of icy reserve. Do not to take too much notice of the lady. The early stages of courtship lay the foundations for one's expectations for married life, and gentlemen who prove their love for a lady by lavishing her with gifts and prattling endlessly of their burning passions will be regarded as no more deserving of authority than a footman, or a lapdog. In such a marriage the lady shall wear the breeches, to the detriment of all concerned.

Ignoring the lady will make her more desirous of pleasing you

ON GENERAL
CONVERSATION.

THERE are few situations more tedious than being expected to furnish nonsense for the ears of particularly dull company. Unfortunately, conversation is commonly regarded as a necessary art of wooing, if only because many ladies set great store by the activity of talking. Contrary to popular estimation, however, this is no excuse for holding forth ceaselessly on nothing at all. Confine yourself to concise, well-timed witticisms and do not waste your breath on the ignorant.

Note the following common mistakes and how they may be corrected:

Egregious Error No. 1: Mumbling, jabbering, or making great, convoluted speeches on matters of no consequence.

Effect: Your company will begin to speculate whether you would be more at home in Bedlam than a Brighton ballroom.

Hint: Your words should be few, and those well-considered before they are delivered. Periods of silence will allow your partner sufficient time to marvel at the mighty intellect that lurks beneath your composed exterior.

Egregious Error No. 2: Being too agreeable.

Effect: Those apt to find something delightful in everything will be thought simple-minded. Those who are too generally agreeable, such as give pleasure to all variety of tempers, should be viewed with strict suspicion.

Hint: With the lady, take care not to let signs of obvious admiration escape you. In general, do not be afraid to express your disdain of your inferiors. Timely reproaches will inevitably excite admiration of your superiority.

Egregious Error No. 3: Introducing ghastly topics of discussion at the dinner-table.

Effect: You will be branded an utter brute and your host will suffer the indignity of the custard trifle going quite untouched.

Hint: Refrain from unreservedly laying before your companions the minutest particulars of your most revolting ailments, an experience of a recent criminal execution/dissection, &c.

Egregious Error No. 4: In debate, conceding the point to your (incorrect) female companion.

Effect: Word of your intellectual defeat at the hands of a mere female will rapidly spread.

Hint: Do not be afraid of pursuing that most satisfying of infernal machines, the 'last word'. As well as being impressed by the intelligence with which you were favoured by nature, she will also be rendered infinitely grateful to you for correcting her misapprehensions.

Egregious Error No. 5: Persisting with conversation that has long since become tiresome, inevitably calling forth the longest stories of the flattest prosers who ever droned.

Effect: Your company will be deluded into thinking themselves agreeable.

Hint: Excuse yourself with a bow and a meaningful glare. The gravity of your departure will persuade all present that they must endeavour to be more interesting if you are forced to cross paths again.

Suitable topics of conversation

IN general, it is rare for ladies to formulate coherent opinions on masculine subjects such as politics, philosophy or other lofty spheres of knowledge. The primary motivations for engaging in conversation with a female are a) to impress her and b) to subject her to a gentle interrogation. All subjects discussed must achieve one of these aims.

Topics designed to please her:

- Inquiries into the health of her family
- The magnificence of your property
- Animals (your own horses, hunting dogs; the number of birds you killed in the last shooting season, &c)

Topics designed to test her:

- Her sharpness of mind: eg. What think you of books?
- Her accomplishments: eg. Do you enjoy music?
- The extent of her connections: eg. And your father, is he happily situated?

The benefits of the latter approach are threefold: a) it affords ample opportunity for examining her suitability, b) she assumes responsibility for most of the conversation, and c) she will appreciate your apparent interest. Every disposition has a tendency to some particular evil, and it is better to know as much as possible of the defects of the person with whom you may consider passing your life. If her faults are trifling, this gives you time correct them; if they are absolute, you may in good conscience abandon all designs upon her.

ON FLATTERY

COMPLIMENTS are appropriate only once you are satisfied that she deserves to be praised (depending on the diligence of your investigation this may take as long as the tenth, or twentieth meeting). Regrettably, many women - even those with no claim to any amiable qualities whatsoever - expect an absurd degree of flattery, but do not degrade yourself by falling into raptures over every aspect of her person. Choose one or two pleasing attributes and express your satisfaction with them in a frank and formal manner. If your lady does not possess beauty, fashion or intelligence - in which case, I am all astonishment at your choice - do not congratulate her for them. Disguise of every sort is the abhorrence of a dignified gentleman, and vanity will be encouraged where there is no qualification for it.

Ladies are seldom flattered by tributes to the extent of their fortune, and few will be won with such compliments as: "Madam, you are so financially well-endowed that I spend all day in the contemplation of your immense riches." If this is truly her only merit I presume that you have elected to marry a widow of advanced years, in expectation of swiftly seizing her financial assets. To such men I offer only this warning: until that day, she will expect some recompense by your services in the marital bed. Think on this for a moment, before escorting her to the altar.

If nothing else is forthcoming consider the following, which are seldom complimented but may nevertheless be thought agreeable feminine attributes:

- the happy alignment of her teeth

- the neatness of her skirts

- the symmetry of her form

- her skills in domestic economy

A few gentle reproaches about her conduct or appearance made within earshot may occasionally be employed as an encouragement to her to improve herself for your benefit.

The Dangers of Studied Compliments

With ludicrous examples from the pen
of the Revd W. Collins

THOSE too dim-witted to pluck flattering remarks from the ingenuity of the moment are fond of wasting their private hours in composing and committing to memory convoluted epistles to imaginary ladies. During my last visit to Rosings Park I was unfortunate enough to be afforded some insight into such a preposterous project. Chancing to find some discarded notes by the chimney-piece in one of the drawing-rooms, and believing them to betray details of some new financial scheme of Colonel Fitzwilliam, I degraded myself so much as to stoop to pick them up. I was mortified to discover the inane amatory ramblings of my Aunt Catherine's latest charitable undertaking, a clergyman by the name of Collins. Some women quarrel with no compliments, however stupidly bestowed, but I daresay such an attack will guard this gentleman's courtship from any charm whatsoever.

I send my unreserved condolences not only to the ladies who find themselves on the receiving end of his affections, but also to the whole village of Hunsford, who will shortly find themselves mortified by his appointment as curate. I include below the contents of the note for your instruction in the kind of unpleasant addresses sure to kill the esteem of any lady.

Complimenting with delicacy, W. Collins

- Madam, the sweet scent perfume of your breath informs me, that your Mother fed on roses, when she begot you

- By your absence, madam, you will deprive [insert location or event] of its brightest ornament

- Your sparkling eyes appear as bright and charming as two quarries of diamonds

- ~~Your noble forehead is like a rock of alabaster~~

- Your delicate form so ~~enchants~~ ravishes beholders that you seem a heavenly creature trapped in a mortal carcass

- If ever you were to leave [insert name of neighbourhood] I feel sure the very trees would bow with grief at your absence

- It has been many years since I have seen such an exemplary [insert name of talent/food/article of furniture]

- Your golden hair appears on your head like ~~the sun~~ flaming amber

- Madam, the magnetic stone observes not the North Star with more alacrity than I do your commands

- Your virtues and perfections – [list the lady's virtues] – cannot fail to arouse the most violent of attachments

THE RUDIMENTS OF DANCING

PEOPLE of all ranks derive an unfathomable degree of enjoyment from dancing, which amounts to little more than flinging one's limbs about a crowded room and being obliged to make physical contact with whomsoever one chances to stand alongside. Nevertheless, as the accomplishment most calculated to display a fine form and graceful carriage it is necessary to dwell on the subject briefly. Before exhibiting yourself in such a manner ensure that you have devoted sufficient study to the exercise. If all onlookers are not overcome with admiration for your expertly turned foot and manly poise, the whole wretched affair has been vain.

An overenthusiastic dancer shames himself at quadrille

Do not be deceived into presuming that the matter should be treated lightly just because it is commonly considered a form of entertainment. A gentleman must request the favour of a lady's hand - do so with grave propriety, ensuring that she is conscious of the honour she has received. Fortunately, it is highly improper for an unengaged lady to refuse. Escort her to the centre of the room with all due precision. When the dance begins, move with grace and purposeful deliberation; carefree abandon will not only jeopardise your dignity, but also the safety of those around you.

Talking to your partner is quite unnecessary - indeed, conversation will distract her from how very fine you look. Instead, fire her heart with respect and admiration by an occasional stern glance in her direction.

Refusing to Dance: A Gentleman's Prerogative

Before committing to the exercise, survey the room. If anybody in attendance appears to suffer from a communicable skin disease, avoid the whole business at all costs. The assumption that gentlemen should not stand 'idle' in a ballroom when ladies are left without dancing partners is impudent and absurd, for the following reasons:

• Females finding themselves without a partner have clearly been overlooked because of some personal deficiency, for which they alone are responsible. Men disinclined to dance should not be forced to do so with the least eligible ladies in the room.

- By preferring to exercise his mind in the contemplation of noble thoughts, the gentleman is clearly engaged in an infinitely more constructive pursuit.

- Females may be more easily admired if there are men solely dedicated to the business of observing them.

Thus, you need not feel obliged to stand up with a partner who is obviously beneath you. A stiff bow and a grimace will suffice as a clear rejection of her company. However, if you are in need of a short line to extricate yourself from this tedious social convention, employ one of the following:

- "I think not - there is no lady here half handsome enough to tempt me"

- "I am currently engaged with contemplating the sheer immensity of my riches"

- "I must decline, for the sake of my health - my physician warns me against the sort of excessive *exhilaration* that the activity would surely bring"

- "It would be an unusual decision, would it not, to elect to dance, when I may from my current position admire the figures of all ladies in attendance at once?"

GIFTS & TRINKETS

THE first pangs of love inspire gentlemen to make all kinds of foolish presents, and most women will beg for more once she is sensible of his attachment. For this reason it is unwise to treat her too freely, or to begin wooing a lady shortly before her birth-day - the project will quickly descend into ruinous expenditure.

While giving gifts ensures success with a particular type of female - just as a dog will favour any man who gives it treats - her interest will wane when pretty trinkets are no longer forthcoming. However, there are certain, sensible gifts that one may bestow upon a lady without encouraging impertinent expectations or utterly violating the codes of decency.

Entirely Appropriate Presents:

- Edifying books
- Poetry or music (generally considered the food of love)
- Hints towards improving herself
- Time in your presence

Utterly Inappropriate Presents:

- Jewellery
- Items of clothing
- Money
- Living things (lap-dogs, horses, domestic servants)
- Lock of your hair, miniature of yourself or similarly intimate items

ON ANIMALS

And how they may endear you to a lady

THE female heart will be immediately softened towards any man who appears pleased with the company of animals (providing, of course, that the animal in question is pretty, or otherwise pleasing to behold - no lady was ever charmed by a spider). The creature, then, must be well chosen, and your manner of handling it in her presence carefully orchestrated.

Likely to inspire affection:

• *Horses:* Provide her with the opportunity of marvelling at your masterly horsemanship. There are few sights so piercing to a lady's heart than a gentleman riding gallantly by on a noble steed, with his coat billowing majestically behind him.

• *Dogs*: Any man who tolerates the whining of a lady's dog will be infinitely preferred, especially if the creature takes the liberty of lying on his lap, or boots (the same may also be said of a widow's infant children). Be aware that some ladies carry small canines around in their silk reticules. Do not suffer the same fate as the Earl of B--l, who immediately fell from favour when he mistook his mistress's beloved Pookie for a wild rat and promptly threw both bag and beast from the window of their chaise. The suit did not end well.

• *Cats*: It will be particularly propitious to endear yourself to cats if you hope to woo a widow, or a confirmed spinster. The great majority appear to derive great comfort from surrounding themselves with an army of feline companions.

• *Exotic menageries*: Now grown fashionable among those with more money than taste. Certainly a useful means of attracting females to one's house, if nothing else can draw them there.

Ladies charmed by the production of a parrot

Unlikely to inspire affection:

- *Pigs, cows, sheep &c*: The rustic classes often embrace their livestock into the family home, before eventually introducing them to the dinner-table. I do not care to speculate whether this is a matter of economy or mere thick-headedness. Whatever the case, forming attachments to farmyard animals in such a manner is not to be encouraged among people of quality.

- *Insects, snails &c*: Creatures that are offensive to behold will only disgust ladies. Lord Erskine delights in producing his pet leeches - named Cline and Home - at the dinner-table, to the horror of his female guests. This curious affection between man and worm will be of little service in his search for a new wife.

HINTS ON
CORRESPONDENCE

AN expertly composed letter has the capacity to convert an indifferent sort of regard into a violent and unreserved adoration. Of course, a regular correspondence would be considered quite improper prior to any actual engagement, but should you have a genuine justification for privately communicating with a lady on occasion nobody's honour shall be injured by it (unless you lose your senses utterly and disclose something entirely improper).

The power of the letter is twofold: a) your words may be carefully chosen, and b) she may revisit the missive at her leisure – with each reading bringing something new and enchanting to her notice. In this way a lady may fall in love with you almost by her imagination alone.

Rules of Correspondence

1. Under no circumstances attempt to communicate with the lady when your intellect has been dulled or destroyed entirely by brandy. Such reckless behaviour is always cause for regret the following morning – once sent, it cannot be unsent. And your handwriting will be monstrous.

2. First professions of love in this form are ill-advised - if her character has been misjudged, you open yourself to an even more mortifying kind of public ridicule than that of one lady: that of several ladies, their mothers, their servants, their servants' friends... &c.

3. Weigh your words well, particularly if you are apt to be run away with your feelings - a man truly in love will write only nonsense.

4. Deliver by hand - preferably your own, but alternatively that of a trusted manservant - to ensure safe receipt. The aforementioned skills in lurking about her house will prove invaluable here.

5. Conclude the note with a vague insult followed by a formal wish for her health and happiness. Such a one cannot fail to inspire reverence.

READING THE SIGNS

With a brief note on discovering a lady's favour by magical means

SOME importunate gentlemen are so intent on advancing their suit that they neglect to confirm whether or not their attentions are agreeable *to the lady*. Unless your perfections are united in such a happy manner as to make you utterly *irresistible*, some small effort should be made to divine whether your labours are being rewarded.

There are persons who, labouring under a particularly peculiar species of imbecility, hope by superstitious or magical means to discover whether their attections are reciprocated. Not being the sort of gentleman to gladly suffer the follies and failures of others, I feel bound to publicly condemn the practice. As these love spells and divinations normally depend upon the unpleasant and time-consuming acquisition of doves' dung, crabs' eyes and dried frogs' tongues, I pity the aspiring suitor almost as much as the frog whose life was destined to end in such ignominious circumstances.

Signs that your attentions are pleasing:

1. She becomes flushed and confused in your presence, and speaks in disorder
2. She is overwhelmed by her passions, and speaks not at all
3. She pays increasing attention to her appearance, and allows you to call her by her first name
4. Sighing, languishing and - if I may speak boldly - heaving of the bosom
5. Weeping with joy at your presence

Signs that your attentions are displeasing:

1. Indelicate or abusive language
2. You are obliged to chase her about the room to continue your conversation
3. Your suggestions for how she may improve her appearance are taken very ill
4. Her maid insists that she is not at home; yet you can spy her hiding in the drawing room
5. Weeping with dismay at your presence

Of course, one need not abandon all hope just because the lady is initially disinclined to receive your favours. I shall reveal how to alter a woman's opinion in chapter V.

FLIRTATION

THE unspoken languages of flirtation are many and various - I expend no energy on performing them and I heartily recommend that you follow my example. However, if your companion begins to exhibit curious behaviour - such as thrusting her parasol in the air or balancing her gloves flat over her face for no discernible reason - she may be attempting to communicate some secret message. Using the guide below you may ascertain what she is trying to say - then instruct her to desist from such absurdity directly.

Deranged behaviour?
She may be flirting

With Gloves

Yes - Crushing up in the left hand
No - Crushing up in the right hand
I love you - Dropping both gloves
Kiss me - Pulling on her right glove, leaving her
thumb exposed
Indifference - Pulling on her left glove half way
Follow me - Striking her gloves on her shoulder
I am engaged - Throwing them up in the air
We are watched - Laying them over her eyes
Get rid of your friend - Folding them up
You have insulted me - Slapping them sharply
across your face

With a Handkerchief

Yes - Holding it to her right cheek
No - Holding it to her left cheek
I am free with my favours - Drawing
it across her lips
I love you - Drawing it across her cheek
I hate you - Drawing it through her hands
You have changed - Holding it to her right ear
We are watched - Drawing across her forehead
I love another - Twisting it in her right hand
I am engaged - Winding it around her finger
Your company is intolerable - Ripping it into pieces

With a Parasol

Yes - Touching her right cheek
No - Touching her left cheek
I am so delighted I can barely contain myself -
Launching it into the air
I wish your acquaintance - Carrying it open in her
left hand
You interest me - Tapping her chin with its handle
You have angered me - Thrusting it towards you
and scowling
Kiss me - Handle to her lips
I love another - Swinging it coyly on her right side
Introduce me to your friend - Biting the tip
*I have observed that you
are looking at another woman* - Placing the tip on
your foot and leaning heavily onto it

ON ATTENTIONS TO OTHER WOMEN

IN love affairs, no woman has a particle of pity for another. Experience informs me that neither is any woman who considers herself within grasping distance of a proposal in possession of 'sound mind'. This unhappy combination generally brings forth all manner of vexation for the man upon whom she has fixed her hopes, whether he realises it or not. You must, therefore, take the strictest care in your dealings with the fair sex, lest your attentions be incorrectly interpreted.

If you are courting:

• All attentions to other women will be conceived as improper, and you will be branded an abominable scoundrel by society.

Once you have resolved to cultivate the affections of one particular female, hold dear the maxim that nothing can clear a man of the iniquitous crime of appearing to admire another lady, no matter how innocent or reasonable his motives.

Objections will be raised to any or all of the following:

1. Flirtation
2. Prolonged conversation
3. Appearing to be amused
4. Dancing with a particular female more than once
5. Making contact with a lady's eyes, or indeed any other part of her person

While rousing a little jealousy in the breast of your beloved can be of service, be careful not to enrage the creature. A woman's imagination is very rapid. Just as it may jump from admiration to love, and love to matrimony before barely a moment has passed, so an affable glance towards another woman may promptly be interpreted as an ardent profession of illicit desire. It is vain to attempt to understand this phenomenon; we must simply acknowledge that it exists and accept that we will be wounded by it.

If you are not courting:

•   Attentions carelessly bestowed on any woman may be mistaken for an expression of preference, and your engagement will be publicly announced before you have been so much as consulted in the matter.

A certain species of excitable lady fondly imagines that a thousand men are dying for the blessing of her hand, when in fact not an individual has yet conceived the slightest impression in favour of her person. In this way the fates of hundreds of men are sealed each year. Without the courage or conviction to deny an attachment - perhaps for fear of causing offence or perhaps from mere idleness - they find themselves expeditiously dragged to the altar by the lady and her grateful parents.

In all, the lesson is this: be careful upon whom you bestow your attentions. Do not waste time in attempting to decipher the workings of the female intellect - we cannot hope to comprehend it. As far as I can divine, it is almost entirely engaged with thoughts of weddings, muslin, the movements of the local militia and how she may contrive to make as many of them as possible fall in love with her at the shortest possible notice.

ON ROGUISH
BEHAVIOUR

For the benefit of both sexes

YOUNG ladies of fashion, who are apt to interpret every look as a declaration of love, are easy prey for dissolute and unfeeling male flirts. Furthermore, and quite contrary to all behaviour that could be deemed rational, many females actually pass over reasonable men in favour of one whose only boast is that he has made for himself a name for intrigue.

Having examined with interest the characteristics that such females find appealing, it seems that there are few men so irresistible as one who considers himself a man of great importance, provided it is in matters of no real consequence. One who makes himself talked of, whether it be for the cock of his top hat, or for loudly prattling in the boxes at the theatre, is in a fair way of being a particular favourite with the ladies. Reckless driving, a striking ruggedness or exotic appearance, and studied indifference to propriety have all done frequent execution upon the sex. Most successful of all these devices, however, is perhaps that of seizing any opportunity to appear before the lady with his attire somewhat in disarray, and some noble (but generally counterfeit) excuse for it – a jacket might be ripped in a scuffle over a lady's honour, or a shirt might be dampened in performing the rescue of a careless kitten from a nearby lake. One is forced to wonder at the peculiarities of the female mind, when such fatuous achievements inspire such unblinking admiration.

A recent affair of dishonour compels me to include a cautionary note on male conduct. With the intention of illustrating the manipulative arts by which some dissipated brutes attempt to ingratiate themselves into the affections of respectable women - whether to plunder their fortune or their chastity - I enclose a crude broadside still in circulation around the most sordid parts of town. The author, I regret, is the very same George Wickham with whose fortunes I seem bound. This work - the fruit of his many enlightening tours of Covent Garden, no doubt - was penned as a means of amusing the young Lord Byron out of his violent amour for a Miss Chaworth. The notorious and debauched career of that young man in the intervening years is perhaps the most persuasive testament to the immorality of its sentiments.

Gentlemen, consult these hints only with a view to appreciating how *not* to attack a reputable female (if you only hope to succeed with a *disreputable* female, a jangle of the purse should do the trick).

Ladies, forgive the alarming nature of the article that follows; I hope your nerves will withstand the exercise of reading it at least long enough to allow for some edification. If you are ever addressed in such a manner, drop all acquaintance with the wretch at once; his good intentions are not to be credited.

THE ACCOMPLISHED FLIRT
by Mr G. Wickham.
Printed in London, 1805

Being the chief arts of seduction, compiled by a notorious philanderer, for the benefit and amusement of novices in matters of the heart, at the particular request of Lord Byron.

***

PART ONE: The Art of Seduction

- Procure a military uniform by any means possible; it is an immense auxiliary towards success with the frivolous and giddy of the sex

- If you find yourself sat near a ravishing beauty at a play or ball, gently press your knee against her back, or touch her leg by accident, in order to have an opportunity of making an apology and showing your gallantry with a bow

- Fabricate a melancholy history to gain her sympathies. If you cannot summon a dead parent or sibling, a tyrannical guardian or deceitful lover will do just as well

- Make expert use of sighs and languishing looks; read long by night and study to be pale - she will be charmed by your melancholy aspect, believing herself to be the cause

- Indulge her vanity - compare her to Helen of Troy, Cleopatra, Juliet; sigh that you are captivated by her 'dove-like eyes' *&c, &c.*

- Intersperse flatteries with merry discourse, and at every opportunity squeeze her hands, play with her hair... and attempt to kiss her until her ears rack!

- Gain the trust of her closest maidservant, who may be easily won with false promises or presents. If rejected by the mistress, console yourself in the arms of the maid!

- Fill your lady's ears with themes of passion. Talk constantly of the violence of your affection; you may 'broil in the flames of most ardent adoration', your heart may be 'full of fire and flame' *&c, &c.*

- Cause her to forget her chaperone - nay! her wearisome virtue! - with talk of parties and adventures. If you can arrange it, a trip in a hot-air balloon is a most exhilarating method of escaping prying eyes, and the experience will leave her *clinging to you* for dear life!

- If all else fails, the addresses of local ladies willing to submit to your pleasure (for a small price) can procured from a number of taverns in Covent Garden

- Convince all ladies in your company of the unequivocal merits of the many *kissing games* to have been imported from France in recent years

Baiser à la Capucine

***

PART TWO: Lines Useful in Charming a Lady

"Lady, I am but a poor fly burnt in the candle of your beauty"

"Who but a man without a heart can behold you and not adore you?"

"Madam, the cannon of your beauty has played incessantly on the citadel of my affections!"

"My sweet, your breasts are as a pair of maiden, unconquered worlds, two soft pillows of love..."

"Fairest of all thy sex, conquered by your bright eyes, I come to offer up my captive heart a victim at your feet!"

"If any tender pity lodges in that snowy breast, allay the storms of my raging passion and let me ravish a kiss from your hand!"

"Come, why will you be an enemy to yourself, and let modesty keep you in this state of Virginity? Oh fair one, I come to offer my service to help you of this trouble..."

"I do adore you, and if you would only licence my hand to stray about, I should be the happiest of men!"

Once you have tempted her to your bedchamber...

"I hope you are confident in me, that my intents are fair and noble? For I shall not offend you with attempting anything that may tend to your disgrace!"

[once she is appeased, attempt something]

"Damn me if you aren't the most beautiful girl I ever laid my eyes, on; and damn me, if I couldn't be tempted to fall desperately in love with you! Do be a good girl, and live with me as my mistress?"

... and the suit is over!

⋆⋆If *maidens* are not to your taste, might I suggest the following publication:

Approved Methods of Conducting an Intrigue with a Married Woman, to which is added, hints towards Alienating the Affections of Unwanted Mistresses, by F. Tilney.

Gentlemen, *outswagger them all!*

G.W.

WHAT IS REQUIRED OF THE FEMALES?

WOMEN are a decorative sex. In general, they have little to say; but what they do say must be said charmingly. In courtship as in most situations, a female need not do anything but look handsome, and express gratitude for all attentions bestowed upon her [note: the only excusable display of indelicate exertion to any degree in a female is when in the act of bearing a child, although this should be minimised as far as possible so as to avoid causing any vexing interruptions to the husband's busy schedule/prior engagements/game of billiards].

Naturally, those enjoying the largest allowance of beauty will inevitably receive the larger share of male attention. But even ladies who cannot boast a fair face may nevertheless find *happiness*, provided they accept that they are unlikely to marry extraordinarily *well*. To a mere farmhand, a wife may atone for her unfortunate face with exceptional culinary capabilities, just as a lady with a pleasing countenance but some slowness of mind may render a gentle widower perfectly happy in his dotage.

My advice to the female quarter on this point is simple: refresh your knowledge of the precepts of attractiveness laid down in chapter II, study hard to be accomplished and sit patiently until a suitable man pays you his compliments.

CHAPTER V

The Proposal

A ND now, reader, you must prepare for the conquest of all that remains unsubdued of her heart. You have reached the culmination of your endeavours: the moment at which the lady is informed of her impending nuptials. Of course, it is unwise to hazard a proposal until you are tolerably well assured of being accepted, but if you have obeyed my instruction thus far, hopes of a favourable conclusion are almost certain. Nevertheless, remain on your guard - an ill-timed fit of amorous enthusiasm may kill your suit at the last moment. Take heart: the whole tedious business - the endless public appearances, the monstrously stupid quizzing, the common-place nonsense talked, the ribaldries passed off as wit, the gallantries, the promiscuous advances of unsightly females and the constant competition as to the manly aspect of one's sideburns - is almost over. You are soon to be engaged, whereupon you may cast off the misery of an uncertain future, and immerse yourself in all the misery of a man in pursuit of matrimonial happiness.

To conclude the counsels, I reveal the most convincing methods of attack and what to expect from the lady's reaction. As the proposal is the only point in the proceedings at which the female party may assume an active role, it is equally important that she is attentive to observing the proper codes of conduct. For this purpose I also offer some direction in how to accept a worthy suitor - and how to crush the hopes of an unworthy one.

A note on displays of emotion

EXCESSIVE displays of feeling are a peculiarly French trait - no doubt inspired by the same regrettable impulse that compels them to bake their sticks of bread into such a promiscuous shape - and as such they have no place on our shores. I notice with distaste, however, that a set of prominent young writers threatens to drag the nation into an age prizing love-stricken melancholy. As a result, I daresay future generations will be so preoccupied with blasted heaths and dead leaves that they shall neglect to get on with shooting at partridges, commissioning attractive portraits of themselves, riding about town in an extremely tall hat and other useful employments of a gentleman's time. Mr Bingley informs me that my opinions are clearly those of a man who has never been in love - I presume he uses the word according to the present universally received sense of the phrase, by which it is applied to every object for which we conceive a passing fondness - and I thank G-d he may be right. I am glad of it, if that is what befalls those who fall in love! It is quite beneath the dignity of an Englishman to allow such a thing.

Crucially, reader, if you are reckless enough to lose your heart, I entreat you not to make the rest of society sick as a result. Be assured that the world has no interest whatsoever in your apparently interminable failures in the realms of eating or sleeping, and will be positively infuriated by your inability to talk any sense whatsoever.

A note on love at first sight

Can one really be stricken with love on a first acquaintance?
Are lovers matched together in Heaven, or is any man
destined to place his affections on a certain female at some
period in his life?

No.

APPLYING FOR CONSENT

IT is no longer necessary to apply first to the lady's father; indeed, if both parties are of age, one need not apply to him at all. However, prior to the proposal it is vital to establish by some subtle inquiry a notion of the dowry likely to be settled on her, at the very least.

The match will be welcomed if it improves the family's social position, in which case you need not trouble yourself too much with reconciling him to the idea. If, on the contrary, your personal shortcomings or haziness of financial prospects prove to be some obstacle, he must be handled with delicacy.

Hints towards dealing with an obstreperous future in-law

Do:

1. Respectfully inform him that you are bound by affection and honour to uphold your promises to his daughter and that the decision lies with her (ensure first that the daughter will comply)
2. Justify your suit in plain and manly terms
3. Enunciate
4. Maintain your composure
5. Pursue designs for acquiring great wealth with renewed vigour

Do Not:

1. Mumble
2. After a quick calculation of his life expectancy, resolve simply to delay your wedding until his objections die with him. His daughter may lose her charms in the intervening years
3. Retort that his consent is quite beside the point in any case, and storm out threatening revenge
4. Weep uncontrollably and beg for his approval
5. Ask if he would be willing to relinquish to you any of his younger or less beautiful daughters

DECLARING YOUR INTENTIONS

AND so, the moment has arrived. Your future wife has been selected and tested, and it only remains to inform her of your intentions. Some say that the greatest art and amorous creativity is to be used in the first declaration of love. On the contrary, as the event is every bit as serious as the purchase of a prize-winning racehorse, it merits just as much gravity. You must:

- Choose the location wisely
- Strike the right tone
- Select your words carefully, approaching the topic in a business-like manner

Location Most importantly, ensure that the business is conducted in private - impudent interruptions when one is trying to concentrate are most off-putting. Otherwise, the location is of little significance, providing it is not ridiculous - it is most disturbing to hear tidings of sentimental couples professing devotion to one another while lurking at their mothers' graves and other such nonsense.

Tone Do not whiningly beseech the pleasure of her hand, but lay before your partner the reasons behind your proposal and the practical advantages to both parties. Her natural inclination to trust the reasoning of the superior male intellect will lead her to reach the same conclusion. Some advise inclining your proposal to the humour of the lady, for example addressing a merry girl as if the whole enterprise was a capital joke. However, there can be no better mode of procedure than approaching the subject with solemnity and regimented self-control.

Words The whole affair ought to be conducted in as few words as possible. To enchant her without nauseating her, and to assure her of your affection without alarming her, they must be carefully chosen. If you will insist on soliciting the hand of a social inferior, outline in no uncertain terms the condescension that you are making, so that she may appreciate your regard even more. In all cases heighten your manly attractions by informing her of your attempts to suppress your feelings. Conclude your address with a fixed and self-assured stare, and express your satisfaction at the prospect of being soon united.

The following expressions are perfectly suitable:

- "I do truly tell you, that I have placed my affection wholly upon you."

- "My heart experiences a fullness and anxiety that can proceed from nothing less than the tenderest and most ardent love."

- "I can no longer restrain the expression of what tender regard I entertain towards you."

- "Madam, to be plain, and without ceremony, I am come to wait on you and offer you my service as a husband."

The following words are not permitted:

- Desire, pleasure, beg, thrust, yearn, loins

Once your address is concluded it is generally necessary to wait a moment for the lady to avail herself of the opportunity to accept. If the lady is of higher standing than yourself, you may need to prepare for some interrogation as to your financial prospects. If you must, prepare beforehand and frame your case to its best advantage (with as unstudied an air as possible).

ON RECEIVING A PROPOSAL
Hints for the Ladies

F EW ladies exhibit much discernment in their methods of securing a husband. The appellation 'Mrs' sounds very well, they think, as they pronounce it; and after arranging their ribbons, petticoats and ringlets to their satisfaction, they consider which man to captivate in order to become secure and independent at the shortest notice.

The moment a lady receives a proposal of marriage will be the defining point of her life, but this does not allow free licence to follow the philosophy of putting her own happiness first. No young woman ought to bestow her affections in a direction that will be disagreeable and inconvenient to her family, and give bad connections to those who have not been used to them. Once you have received a gentleman's compliments, ask yourself the following questions:

- Is his fortune sufficient to support me as I should wish?

- Has his education been such as to qualify him to be a pleasing companion to me?

- If not, can I so far forget my own education as to descend to a level with him?

A man without education and refined sentiment may love you, I admit, but not in a manner that will be agreeable to you; for, as he will not be able to comprehend the extent of your excellence, he cannot know the condescension you make in consenting to squander away your life on a certified ignoramus.

If you mean to accept –
When his suit is over, offer your thanks for the honour he has paid you and promptly acknowledge your readiness to accept his hand, all in the tender and submissive tones befitting genteel femininity. Cruel recourse to testing his affections, holding him in suspense, or other mean arts will betray a lack of feeling that may cause him to reconsider his attack. A silent, unaffected tear of joy and a gentle smile may be pleasing to the gentleman, but do not cause him to regret his suit by unusual gasping, weeping or screeching.

If you are uncertain –
Some further enquiry into his prospects may be advisable. Better to take an hour or so to consider than to reject a man in haste – think on the possibility that another proposal may never be made to you.

For instruction in *refusing a man's proposal* I applied to Miss Maria Bertram, of Mansfield Park. This, of course, is only really of service to ladies of exceptional quality – such a refusal made by a female of lesser standing would be at once pedantic and ill-bred.

Declining a Man's Addresses

by Miss Maria Bertram.

One of the great trials of being an excessively beautiful woman, whose charms also extend to the possession of wealth, is the stream of unsolicited romantic epistles that conspire to render one's days so tiresomely repetitive. Of course, when one enjoys the advantages of moving in polite society one must expect to have one's time thus intruded upon; but there is certainly no reason to waste it on the ugly, or the poor, even in the face of the fearful possibility of being eventually cast aside like an old shoe. It is crucial, therefore, for a lady to understand how to deliver an effective rebuff.

Hints towards refusing an amiable man

• "As my heart is yet my own, and as I am determined to keep it so until I meet with a man whom I shall consider as truly worthy of the sacrifice of my liberty, I must beg leave to decline."

• "I am sorry to cause you pain, but I cannot accept you. If you will excuse me - a little solitude will be agreeable."

• "I beg you will allow me the favour of declining your kind offer; it pains me to inform you that my affections are engaged elsewhere."

Hints towards refusing a persistent man

Some gentlemen may actually be encouraged by the tender tones of such a rejection. If he applies to you again, you must entirely undeceive him.

• "Sir, I have already told you, that I could not love, therefore your further suit is all impertinence; it is as possible that the fixed stars should leave their stations, that I should love you."

• "You are the last man on earth whom I could ever be prevailed upon to marry."

Hints towards refusing an impertinent man

If you suspect that a gentleman hopes you will submit to something you conceive improper, he is likely to express himself in a particularly direct or lascivious manner. Begin with gentle reproaches that remind him of your virtue, and shun him entirely if his unwanted attentions persist.

Begin with:

•   "Sir I beseech you to be more sparing of your courtesies, lest the world take you for a prodigal."

•   "Your advances oblige me to think you don't design me for your wife, and my honesty bids me tell you that I will never be your whore; and therefore, sir, you may desist from further courting, for it will be but lost labour."

If he persists:

•   "I would sooner throw myself into a nunnery than call myself your wife!"

•   "I should think myself unworthy of the character of woman, should I hold any further connection with so base a wretch!"

•   "Unhand me, sir, before I am obliged to call for your removal!"

At the Upper Assembly Rooms in Bath last season I was even obliged to fall into a false swoon to deter the advances of the thoroughly wicked Captain Tilney (indeed, the art of fainting in company - convincingly but with grace - is an important one to perfect). Execrable as the character of this unprincipled debauchee notoriously is, I daresay he does cut a very dashing figure indeed, and is unquestionably possessed of good taste - the ladies were quite in raptures with him. And heir to a large estate too, I am told. I have half a mind to convince my brother Tom to invite him to Northamptonshire; it should be a fine thing to be mistress of an Abbey, I am sure.

Miss Bertram.

IDENTIFYING A
SUITABLE HUSBAND

For the edification of ladies of good stock

The following exercise is designed to test your mastery in the art of detecting whether a gentleman is deserving of your hand. Cast your eyes over the following matrimonial candidates, consider their merits and make your choice. Turn to page 193 to see how you have fared.

Candidate A:

Lieutenant RICHARD ROISTER

Never neglects an opportunity of being charming.

Likes - Driving his curricle at great speed, talking, being talked of, liquor.

Dislikes - The prospect of meeting your parents.

Candidate B:

Mr TOBIAS BUMPKIN

Of little personality and no professional prospects.

Likes – Cavorting with the pigs, wholesome beer.

Dislikes – Long words, bathing.

Candidate C:

Mr ARCHIBALD FOPLING

Distinguished heir of the Macaroni Club.

Likes – The company of men, feathers, ribbons, muslin, being addressed as 'Primrose Poll'.

Dislikes – Marriage, women.

Candidate D:

Mr GEORGE AUGUSTUS HAUGHTEY

An older man of noble bearing.

Likes – Fishing, shooting, swimming in his private lake.

Dislikes – Pointless conversation, dancing, any species of filth, the French.

Candidate E:

Mr HEATHCLIFF

A Gothic hero, not yet in fashion.

*Like*s – Scowling, prowling the Yorkshire moors, getting revenge.

Dislikes – Refined folk, neighbours, acting with propriety.

Answer

The most suitable candidate for matrimony is *D*.

Mr Haughtey is a model of self-control, fortitude and good sensible English values. The marriage will result in wide social acclaim and an impressive progeny of strapping boys.

If you chose:

A – *Mr Roister* is a scoundrel of the first order. A serial ruiner of reputations, he undoubtedly harbours designs on your virtue of the basest kind. If you do marry it shall be at Gretna Green, after which unhappy event he will waste no time in squandering your fortune, and busying himself with impregnating the prettiest of the house staff, and most of your female neighbours.

B – *Mr Bumpkin* clearly belongs to the peasant classes, and should not be paying his addresses to a respectable lady. Even if he is fortunate enough to acquire money, your household will always be rendered conspicuous by the unpleasant odour of rotting potatoes.

C - Mr Fopling is an unusual fellow, and marries you to please his mother. Under no circumstances enquire into the nature of his nightly excursions, unless you wish to scandalise the whole neighbourhood. He will eventually disgrace you both by attempting to seduce one of the footmen.

E - Mr Heathcliff is a predatory lunatic of the most vulgar propensities. If you accept his suit you will suffer a stifling and tormented existence. If you refuse, he will move into the neighbouring estate and spend the rest of his life attempting to wreak his revenge on your children.

IN THE EVENT OF REJECTION

IF he has followed my instructions it is nigh on impossible to conceive of a man who may be declined by a woman of *sense*. Unfortunately, the quality is not distributed liberally among the sex. Thus, it is not necessary to accept a first refusal as final. The female mind is notoriously wavering, and in general their hearts seldom go along with their tongues.

Reacting to rejection

DO NOT:

• Allow your feelings to be puffed about, nor permit your face to betray any sign of discomposure

• Make indelicate retorts or resort to *childish insults*. eg. "No fear, I see no point in doting on so small a stock of beauty as yours!"

• Demand that her father forces the match

• *Rant and rave* and threaten death in various forms

• Attempt to *kill your rival* if you discover that her affections are engaged elsewhere

There is to be no weeping

Acknowledge her response with decency, take your leave and consider her refusal at your leisure. Refer to Miss Bertram's hints to measure how disgusting your suit was to the lady, and identify the reasons for her unfavourable answer. Did she name a particular fault of your character or person that rendered you utterly unmarriageable? If, upon further reflection, you consider her criticisms to be justified, your failings must be corrected. When you next fall into her company, study her countenance and ascertain what degree of dejection the business has produced. If signs are favourable, there is no reason to suppose that you are incapable of prosecuting your second suit with rigour and effect. If, on the other hand, you are truly unable to account for such treatment, then it is reasonable to assume that the fault lies with the lady.

Possible reasons for rejection

1. *The derangement of her mind*

It is quite possible that she is, in plain words, quite
mad. Female hysteria is prevalent among the civilised
orders, and you may be thankful that this lurking
deficiency has presented itself before it became too
late. Being chained in wedlock to a lunatic would be
most inconvenient, and potentially very expensive if
you were compelled to commit her to an institution.

2. *The temporary disorder of her wits, on account of your brilliance*

If she is a lady of marked sensibility or agitated
nerves, she may have been overcome by the dazzling
manner of your proposal and refused you accidentally.
If you are determined to have her for your wife, wait
a short while and pay your compliments again in a
style less likely to alarm her.

3. *She has been impertinent enough to fix her affections elsewhere*

An objection usually voiced by idealistic young ladies.
There is no reason to relinquish all hope: console
yourself with the thought that she may have fixed
her hopes on a scoundrel, or a soldier soon to be
dispatched to the Peninsula. Adopt the aspect of a
concerned friend and ensure that you are constantly

in her thoughts, safe in the knowledge that your rival may soon be disgraced, imprisoned or killed.

4. She means to torment you with feminine tricks

The lady may be exercising her privilege of refusal merely for the sake of it, or perhaps because she labours under the delusion that such trifling will heighten your affection. If her refusal is marked with gentleness and compassion, she may be anxious to avoid being easily won, and nurse hopes that you will prove your love. In this case, accept the challenge. On the contrary, the woman who merely delights in your discomfort is best discarded.

IN THE EVENT OF
ACCEPTANCE

ONCE your suit has been accepted it may be considered agreeable to seal the contract with a chaste kiss, as a sign of your thanks and proof of your honourable intentions. Under no circumstances, however, may you allow yourself to be overrun with emotion. Once you are married such tokens of affection will quickly weaken into nothing more than a morning duty, like the combing of your sideburns or the buttoning of your shirt. It is best not to encourage wild expectations of passionate felicity in a lady, that will only return to annoy you in the persistent overtures of a wife.

Following your engagement, a lady's manner towards you is liable to undergo a rapid and seismic transformation. Her thoughts will be occupied wholly with the nuptials, the parties at which you may broadcast your attachment, pondering the pleasure of her own success and the methods by which she may vex other females with it. A gentleman must tolerate this silly behaviour for a short time. You must also allow her to make an announcement in the newspapers – to the female mind, one may as well be single if the wedding is not to be in print.

CONTRACTING AN UNFORTUNATE ALLIANCE

NEXT to a battle lost, the greatest misery may be a battle gained - particularly if you neglect to profit by my advice and your betrothed proves to be unfit for the purpose. Unfortunately, your only hope of escaping the marriage is if she threatens to disgrace you both through dalliances with other men, or if she falls prey to a fatal disease. In short, you are duty-bound to fulfil your promises to the lady, and may in all legitimacy be forcibly compelled to the office by her family, a quite undignified state of affairs for all concerned. You must simply contrive some way of making the best of a bad bargain, as many generations of men have before you.

The scold's bridle

One may perceive concern about the propriety of marriage even in the most vulgar of circles - even if they have no such regard for the propriety of anything else. In the village of Lambton there were wed two local peasants last month, and when asked whether he would take his partner to be his wedded wife, the fellow replied: "Yes, I'm willin'; but I'd a much sight rather have her sister." At this his bride fell into a swoon, her sister began to congratulate herself most heartily and their mother - shrieking that as he was content to cause a swell in her belly he should be pleased to make her an honest woman - struck him so forcibly about the head as to knock him quite out of his senses. Such are the matrimonial manners of the swinish multitudes.

CONSOLATION FOR THE CONTINUALLY REJECTED

U NRECIPROCATED love is the cause of many a blighted life, and such a one as I should never wish on a person of respectability. However, it is not good form to languish around in such violent paroxysms of self-pity that you live only to be an instrument of annoyance to the rest of the world. Those believing themselves to be martyrs for love make the most insufferable company.

To Bachelors

Sirs, if your matrimonial prospects are utterly exhausted, resign yourself to the fact with the stoicism befitting an Englishman and acquaint yourself permanently with the life of a bachelor. Grey-bearded gallants who pursue young ladies with as much alacrity as a youth of one and twenty are an embarrassment to themselves and an object of ridicule for everybody else.

There is certainly some consolatory prize to be gleaned from your utter failure - you need never be troubled by the vexations of a wife and lawful children. Both serve to deplete a gentleman's funds drastically. Furthermore, infants prove disappointing company for the first few years of their existence, nature having made them little more than machines for the production of incessant babbling, and only ever unintelligible nonsense at that. In fact, they routinely display a stubborn inability to acquit themselves with any social grace whatsoever.

Turn your attentions instead to identifying a male heir for your estate - a nephew, perhaps, or a favourite illegitimate child if you must - and educate them to the position, unless you wish your property to fall into the hands of some ridiculous distant relation.

To Old Maids

Ladies, if you have failed to secure a husband by the age of thirty - at which point the bloom of youth will fade most desperately - admit defeat and harden yourself to the idea of not being worth looking at. A single woman of nine and twenty ought not to expect to feel or inspire real affection again. Do not bemoan the fact that young men only detect in your features the ruins of a face that was once considered handsome and, above all, do not disgust the public by becoming such an abominable maiden ewe as insists on dressing in the fashion of a lamb.

Ageing spinsters appear to occupy themselves solely with embroidery, economising, brushing dust from teapots, sighing, surrounding themselves with cats and entreating any visitors to light a blazing fire in compassion to their creaking bones. Without independent wealth, you shall be a burden to your father, and after his death you shall be a burden to your brothers, perhaps even to their sons, and grandsons. You must reconcile yourself to such a way of life, if you hope ever to be content.

Console yourself with the thought that you shall never suffer the loss of your virtue by the enjoyment of those pleasures that a female may only be acquainted with in the marital bed. If you have been so reckless as to surrender your chastity before wedlock, then I daresay it is utterly unsurprising that nobody has been inclined to take you for his wife. The only option left to you is to contemplate on your disgrace until your dying day.

A maiden ewe, dress'd lamb fashion

A closing message of encouragement from the author

And so, indefatigable reader, you arrive at the end of your lesson.

With the benefit of my matchless instruction, you should be able to pass yourself off with no small degree of credit. If you are deserving of the sentiment, I wish you success - of which you cannot fail if you follow these instructions. If you are not, then I wish you no such thing. Our contract being at an end, I take my leave - with the closing thought that I have no interest whatsoever in being apprised of the outcome of your endeavours. Desist from annoying me with them. If I have any consistency, it is in my thoughts on the matrimonial machinations of others - and I daresay that arises from my abhorrence of the subject altogether.

I bid you good day.

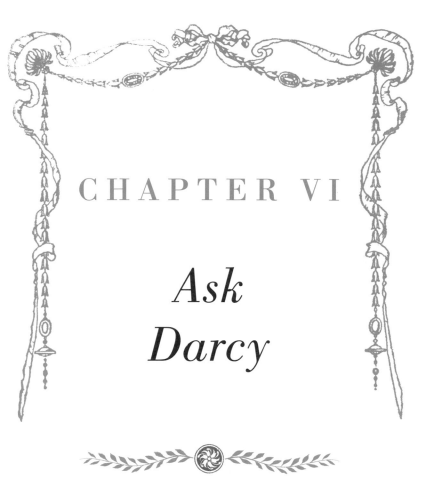

CHAPTER VI

Ask Darcy

In which the author is importuned for his counsel on divers matters of the heart

I INCLUDE in this revised edition of *Mr Darcy's Guide to Courtship* a selection of the more coherent letters desperately addressed - with little thought for propriety - to my estate at Pemberley. Correspondents who did not submit their missives anonymously will, I trust, have no objection to their complaints being published as received, as I have as little compunction to trouble myself on their behalf as they have appreciation of the demands on my time.

Darcy,

I have fought wars, I have battered the scum of the earth into something resembling a competent army, I have seen men blown to pieces before my eyes - but Damn it all if dealings with a woman aren't more troublesome than everything else together!

These past twenty years my wife has grown miserably ugly. Her charms faded before we even reached the altar, but by G-d, sir, I stood by my promise. Though we have repeatedly tried to live in a friendly manner, I find I much prefer the company of prettier women. I fondly imagine that we may be reconciled, if only she would try to fix her appearance. How might I approach the subject with delicacy?

- Wellington

Sir,

I expect your wife is sensible of her physical defects, but perhaps she does not realise how disgusting they are to you. Speak loudly of your dissatisfaction with her appearance to others, ensuring that she hears your reproaches. She will appreciate that you have not offended her modesty by speaking of it to her directly and, compelled by her wifely duty to please you, I have little doubt that she will address the issue of her lost charms with renewed enthusiasm.

FD.

Sir,

I have been captivated by a girl recently moved to Devonshire; we spend blissful hours reading poetry and taking long walks across the country. There is not a man on earth who could withstand such tender beauty! But my aunt threatens to disinherit me if I do not marry more prudently. What should I do?

-Mr. J. Willoughby

Willoughby,

You are clearly suffering the ill effects of a fleeting infatuation. If you have not begun your courtship of the girl in earnest, put an end to it by dropping her acquaintance entirely. The whole affair sounds rather nauseating - as well as pleasing your family by marrying a girl of some importance in the world, she must exhibit some degree of sense if you are to be cured of your ridiculous romantic inclinations.

FD.

Oh, Mr Darcy!

In the Spring Lord Byron confessed an undying passion for me, and we became embroiled in a delicious affair – but now he refuses to see me and I think I shall go mad! He persuaded me to elope with him last month but has since left his poor Caro alone. I have dressed as a boy to gain admission to his apartments, I have tried stabbing myself before his very eyes, I have sent him gifts of my blood and my most intimate hair – yet he refuses me. That beautiful pale face is my fate. But he will not believe it.

My husband is also being dreadfully tedious about the whole thing and threatens to take me off to Ireland. Oh, sir, the world conspires against my love!

– Lady Caroline Lamb

Madam – you are a menace to yourself and all who have dealings with you. You have been false to your husband, a fiend to your lover, and a fine joke to every body else. Learn the proper manners befitting a lady of rank and repent at once.

FD.

Sir,

I am utterly consumed with lust for a young lady of my acquaintance and fear that I shall be the undoing of both of us. How can I control my passions?

– A gentleman

Sir,

The ardour may be cooled by a number of small but effective attentions: eat cold meats, do not enliven your desires with liquor, take a bracing swim in a cold lake, and think of disagreeable female relations – I, for instance, use the example of my Aunt Catherine – when in the presence of your mistress.

FD.

Sir,

I write having been most rudely rejected by an impertinent young gentlewoman after she explicitly encouraged me to believe in her affection. I am incensed by the cruelty of the sex! I begin to fear that my faith in divine wisdom is not strong enough to prevent me from seeking my revenge.

- the Rev. Philip Elton, Highbury

Mr Elton,

However unfeeling and cunning and unfeeling her actions, I cannot condone the defamation of this unnamed lady's character, if she is of noble birth. Injure her pride by securing the hand of one even more elegant, and fire a little jealousy in the heart of your former lover. Take a trip to a town of fashion - Bath, perhaps? - and seek a fortune of your own.

FD.

Sir,

I am mother to five unmarried daughters – oh! five! – with nothing to look forward to but the death of my husband and the destitution of us all! The event of this is all very provoking, and I am so dreadfully afflicted by tremblings and flutterings that I don't know what may become of me. What can be done for my girls? My eldest and my youngest are both uncommonly pretty and agreeable, and if only they could be thrown into the paths of rich men I am quite sure they could find excellent husbands.

– Mrs B., Hertfordshire

Madam,

If your girls truly had merit I daresay that one of them should have secured a husband by now. As they are so clearly slighted by men of distinction you must be blind to their inferior prospects. I daresay you should lower your aim.

FD.

Dear Sir,

I am 42 and utterly enchanted by Sophia, a beautiful teenage courtesan. We are to be married in February, but she exhibits an unqualified dislike for everything about my company, except the presents I can give her. How can I make myself more agreeable?

- The Duke of Berwick

Sir,

I noted the occasion of your marriage with dismay. I am truly sorry to see a gentleman humiliate himself by marriage to a common prostitute. No matter. I am afraid that there is nothing to be done.

FD.

Kind Sir,

I feel I have a thousand things I would ask you – but I will confine myself to one at present. Once my affections have been placed, it is not in the power of anything to change them, and I have lately fixed them on a dashing Captain of very recent acquaintance. He flirts with me outrageously and so fervently do I prefer him to every other man that I begin to believe I shall carry my whim so far as to marry him!

Alas, I have already offered my hand to another. He is quite over head and ears in love with me, but his tiresome parents refuse to allow us any decent sort of living. Having lasted a week without breaking the engagement I commend my own conduct in this affair extremely, but I am more tempted to it every day. Is this terribly wicked of me?

– Miss Belle Thorpe

Miss Thorpe,

I must congratulate you on showing promise to become one of the most accomplished coquettes in England. If you would cast aside your honour and the heart of a good man for a mere flirtation by all means go ahead, but do not be deceived into thinking that any other will take you for his wife.

FD.

Sir,

I have conceived a passion for a local girl of no breeding whatsoever and am quite disgusted by my inability to shake the inclination. The disgrace! Naturally I should never marry her, but I am sorely tempted to install her as my mistress. Would her mere presence pollute the family estate?

- A man of noble standing.

Sir,

Under no circumstances may you make addresses to this girl. Console yourself with the knowledge that as the life expectancy of miserable peasant girls is little above five and twenty, it is unlikely that your torment will last long.

FD.

Sir,

After forty years at sea I am resolved to quit the navy life and settle down. Unfortunately my years of service have rendered me somewhat displeasing to behold – I was robbed of my health in the East Indies and a leg at Trafalgar. I lost my teeth and my good name in a tavern brawl on the Ratcliffe Highway, but that is a separate matter altogether.

How might I persuade a lady to forget my unconventional features so far as to consent to marry me?

Capt. Gavin, Farnham

Sir,

A life at sea is no beautifier, certainly, and refined manners are difficult to cultivate with a head full of rum and a diet more weevil than biscuit.

But, I daresay the profession has equipped you with commendable attributes – a manliness of character, an officer's uniform and bewitching tales of military honour. If companionship is all you seek, a widow of failing eyesight would be most amenable to the idea. Prove that you are a *pure gentleman* in your notions and behaviour, and a female of greater charms may be willing to accept you.

FD.

Sir,

Last year, in a fit of chivalrous folly, I secured myself a wife and a cold on the same day. I got rid of the last pretty speedily, but the elopement has been the source of all sorts of mischief.

My father has treated us ill, vilely, and refuses to receive us on account of my choice of wife; a trusted friend has affronted us both in his attempts to seduce her; now she has insisted on moving her insufferable sister into our conjugal home. I am seriously persuaded that the situation will begin to be injurious to my health; how might I cultivate matrimonial harmony in such wretched circumstances?

P. B. Shelley

Sir,

If your marriage is unlikely to contribute to your felicity, you must learn to distract yourself from your inevitable, looming misery with other concerns.

Devote yourself to the improvement of your mind. Strike up a correspondence with like-minded intellectuals and a take a trip around the continent. While your conduct must at all times remain impeccable, you may indulge your passions through your work – pursue your interest in poetry, perhaps?

FD.

Sir

I have reached the age of five and thirty and begin to lose all hope of ever receiving an offer of marriage. I am led to believe that my appearance is not wholly offensive, and yet no man has even formed designs upon my virtue! Must I forfeit the good opinion of the world and resign myself to spinsterhood?

- Miss K.

Miss K,

I shall forebear to injure your feelings by saying that your prospects are dead, but I am afraid that they are not alive. Your silence on the subject of your wealth persuades me that it is too great for words - there are consolations that spinsterhood can bestow for ladies of fortune. Adopt the role of a chaperone at social events. Instead of exerting yourself in pursuit of a husband you will be ushered onto a sofa next to the fire and may drink as much wine as you like.

FD.

A SELECT BIBLIOGRAPHY

I cannot say I am lucky enough to have seen any fun in compiling this book. Nevertheless, I flatter myself that it could not have been more diligently researched. Some works have proved particularly valuable, as well as various journals - *The Gentleman's Magazine*, *The Spectator*, *The Rambler*, &c &c. By way of thanks to the authors - and should they continue to draw breath they may not expect recompense of any other kind - I lay them before you now.

The Complete Works of Miss Jane Austen
The Academy of Complements, Anon (1645)
The Art of Making Love, Le Boulanger de Chalussay (1676)
The New Art of Courtship, D_n S_t (c.1733)
The Rudiments of Genteel Behaviour, F. Nivelon (1737)
The Amorous Gallant's Tongue, Anon (1741)
A Dictionary of Love, Anon (1777)
The New School of Love, Anon (1786)
Matrimony Made Plain, Easy & Delightful, Anon (1791)
The Lover's Instructor, Anon (1792)
Lavater's Looking-Glass, Johann Kaspar Lavater (1800)
The Miseries of Human Life, James Beresford (1806)
Mirror of the Graces, a 'Lady of Distinction' (1811)